Retire Early, Retire Rich

A Roadmap to Financial Freedom for the Middle-Class

Bradford W. Barber

Copyright © 2018 Bradford W. Barber

All rights reserved.

No part of this book may be reproduced in any form or by any means, electronic or mechanical, including photocopying, recording or by any information storage and retrieval system, without the prior written permission of the Publisher.

Printed in the United States of America

ISBN-13: 978-1986597531

Editing by Zac Nelson

MEET THE AUTHOR

Brad lives with his wife, son, and border collie in Cincinnati, Ohio. He has a Bachelor of Science in Civil Engineering from Ohio Northern University and is a registered Professional Engineer in multiple states. His work experience includes cost benefit analysis, estimating, and analytical studies for multi-million-dollar construction projects.

Brad's journey of financial independence and early retirement started shortly after graduating college. As newlyweds, they began chasing the quintessential American Dream by purchasing their first home (along with a crushing mortgage), two brand new cars, and a mountain of student loan debt. In just a few short years, the young couple managed to accumulate over a quarter million dollars of debt. Together they learned real world lessons on how to cut expenses, pay off their debt, and work towards saving and investing over 70% of their income!

TABLE OF CONTENTS

Chapters	Page #
1: Introduction	1
2: Motivation	3
3: Past & Present	11
4: Debt	15
5: Cutting Expenses	21
6: Income	37
7: Saving	45
8: Assets vs. Liabilities	49
9: Investing	53
10: Home Ownership	75
11: Early Retirement	97
12: Taxes	121
13: Millionaires	125
14: Better Yourself	149
Further Reading	161
Index	163

This publication is designed to provide accurate and authoritative information in regard to the subject matter covered. It is sold with the understanding that neither the author nor the publisher is engaged in rendering legal, accounting, investment, or other professional services. The author is not responsible for any financial loss or liability incurred as a result of the use of any information contained in this book. If legal advice or other expert assistance is required, the services of a competent professional person should be sought.

The names of those interviewed in this publication are pseudonyms.

INTRODUCTION

There is a **BIG** financial secret of which most people are not aware.

Did you know you can retire early, with millions of dollars in net worth, working a white-collar, blue-collar or even a pink-collar job? And it doesn't involve pyramids, scams or schemes.

This book focuses on making smart financial decisions, the strategies needed to grow wealth organically, and tips from real life millionaires. It's less complicated than you might think; personal finance is less about math and more about emotions and behaviors. You don't need a PhD, MD, or any letters in front of or after your name to understand the basic principles this book will teach you. Creating wealth in its simplest form is an aggregate of financial knowledge, hard work, and seized opportunities. The principles you will discover in this book can be used whether you're in your 20s and just getting started in life, or in your 50s and looking to better prepare for retirement. It doesn't matter if you make $30,000 a year or $300,000 a year, there are valuable lessons for everyone.

Far too many wealth creation finance books require you to be out of debt and be willing to take big risks with your money. Others expect you to take out massive loans or a second mortgage to start a business assuming you will automatically be successful. Realistically, half of all businesses fail to turn a profit within the first several years and 96% of businesses won't reach the 10-year mark. It's true that over half of all millionaires are business owners and of course those that do make it are often wildly profitable with fantastic success stories, worthy of the acknowledgment they receive. However, choosing a path of entrepreneurship is not a requirement to become wealthy and is not for everyone. It requires intense dedication and has a high probability of failure, leaving the creator saddled with mountains of debt or even forced into bankruptcy.

Other books offer up wealth creating strategies such as get-rich-quick schemes that involve a dishonest individual separating an innocent person from their hard-earned money.

Don't be fooled! Any middle-class American can achieve great wealth and be able to retire early.

Unfortunately, personal finance is rarely taught in high school or even college. As a result, most people learn how to handle money through trial and error, where wisdom is only gained after real world mistakes, and often with big financial consequences. Instead of waiting to learn from your mistakes, arm yourself with the financial knowledge needed to win with money the first time!

I hope you enjoy reading this book as much as I enjoyed writing it, and that it helps turn your financial dreams into reality.

-Bradford W. Barber

MOTIVATION

"The road to success isn't easy to navigate, but with hard work, drive and passion, it's possible to achieve the American dream."
– Tommy Hilfiger

In recent decades, it has become socially acceptable for people to not take responsibility for their actions, and expect others, such as their government or the company for which they work, to care for them. Passing on this burden rids them of the difficult responsibilities of adulthood, but also means they give up control of their financial freedom and allow others to define their dreams and what the future holds.

Fortunately, the American Dream is still alive and well; it just takes a lot of hard work to achieve, like it did generations ago for our parents and grandparents. The only thing that changed is the entitlement attitude among some in our culture. Most people don't worry about retirement because they feel it's so far away, or that its someone else's responsibility, but life goes by quickly and not planning for the future is just as bad as intentionally planning to fail.

Regardless of personal situations or what stage of life you are in, you must define clear financial goals and find the motivation necessary to follow through with them. Dreams only become reality when you take action to achieve them.

Goals

First start by outlining a set of goals, then seek out the purpose and motivation necessary to achieve them. It's important that the goals be tangible and realistic. Saying you want to save up $500,000 in one year when you only make $100,000 a year is not realistic, but if you change the timeline to ten years, it then becomes achievable.

Retire Early, Retire Rich

Put your goals in writing and tell others (a spouse, family member, friends or even a co-worker) what they are. We often dream big, but rarely do we follow through as obstacles along our path make achieving our goals difficult. Rather than work through it, we give up. Failure becomes easier when you're the only one who knows, but telling others your goals can help keep you accountable and encourage you to follow through. By sharing your goals, you allow others to encourage you, keep you motivated, and help make them a reality. For instance, if you're trying to pay off credit card debt and are looking to pick up extra work, someone may know of a business that is hiring part time on the weekends, allowing you to pay off the debt faster. Or if they know you want to build a deck on your home, maybe they have a family member who is a contractor and can help you complete the project for a fraction of what other contractors are asking.

When putting together a list of your goals, be sure to visualize what you are working for. Don't just write it on a piece of paper and forget about it. Visualization is a powerful motivation tool, especially for long-term goals, which can be years away and very expensive, such as buying a home, taking a dream vacation, or paying for your children's college education. Start by incorporating all of your senses and allowing yourself to see, hear, taste, smell, and feel what it is you desire. This will make it seem more real and actually obtainable!

Visualization will give you the laser sharp focus needed to create the emotional drive necessary to achieve your goals. If you're saving for a vacation, start by watch videos online of where you want to go, find what hotel you will stay in, listen to the waves lap on the white sandy beach, imagine the warmth of the sun on your skin, feel the the sand between your toes, and see the beautiful colors in the sky as the sun sets. If you're looking to buy a home, go to open houses for encouragement. If your goal for financial independence is to help others, start by volunteering at homeless shelter or other charities to remind yourself what you are working for and that one day you will be able to donate more than just your time.

Short-term goals are small inexpensive tasks that can be completed in as little as a few weeks or months, and often look more like a to-do-list than a series of lofty hopes or dreams. Some examples include:

- Saving up an emergency fund
- Paying off credit card debt
- Starting a 401(k) or 529 Plan
- Repairing a vehicle

Mid-term goals are larger more expensive goals that may take several months or up to a few years to complete. Some examples include:

- Paying off an auto loan
- Saving up the down payment for a home
- Upgrading a kitchen or bathroom

Long-term goals are the most expensive and time-consuming goals and often take years or even decades to achieve. Some examples include:

- Paying off your mortgage
- Putting a child through college
- Paying for a wedding
- Having $1,000,000 or greater invested in a 401(k)
- Buying a vacation home
- Leaving a legacy that will last generations

If you have already taken the time to come up with clear and well-defined goals, but are still struggling to save money, stay out of debt, or feel your goals are not worth the sacrifice, then your goals are not adequate. Dreams worth pursuing will provide you with the motivation and drive necessary to following through.

If your child or family member was sick and needed a life-saving surgery in one year, but it was going to cost $15,000, nothing would stop you from coming up with the money. You wouldn't sleep until you came up with a plan. Small goals may require small sacrifices, but big meaningful goals will provide the emotional drive necessary to follow through and make those big sacrifices.

Working Together

For those who are married, it's vital to be on the same page with your spouse. They say opposites attract, but personal finance is one area where both partners need to be aligned. When one person is a saver and the other is a spender, it creates a source of conflict making marriage difficult, developing a constant source of tension, and is a leading cause of divorce. When spouses work together as a team, they can save and grow wealth more quickly than as individuals. The sum of the couple is more than the individual persons. With financial problems being one of the leading causes of fights and divorces, taking a path toward financial independence and early retirement often has the hidden benefit of increasing communication and creating a happier and healthier marriage.

Purpose

The modern middle-class family lives a busy hectic lifestyle, where they tackle one day at a time, rarely looking into the future more than a week or two in advance. When getting out of debt and saving for the future, it helps to take a step back and look at the bigger picture. View life not as something you are experiencing right here, right now, but as a journey with many stages and adventures.

Imagine yourself in the window seat of an airplane getting ready to take off. As the plane accelerates down the runway, you lean your head over to look out the window. As the plane leave the ground, you notice how everything that was near you seconds ago quickly becomes smaller and fades into the distance. By time you reach 10,000 feet, individual trees, roads, cars, homes, and even stadiums are nearly invisible. From this altitude, you only notice large terrain features, such as rivers, lakes, fields, forests, and mountains. Now take a minute to view your life from 10,000 feet.

What important events do you see?

It might be your first car, graduating high school, going to college, your wedding, your first home, the birth of a child or grandchild, adopting a pet, taking a family vacation, or retirement. Notice how small everyday activities and expenses, such as dining out, buying that big screen TV or going to the movies are infinitesimal and do nothing to define your journey or who you are. Most middle-class Americans spend an excessive amount of money on everyday "inexpensive" items that steal a large percentage of their wealth, add little or no value to their lives, and prevent them from achieving their major financial and non-financial life goals. Seeing the bigger picture makes small purchases seem less important and will help you save for the bigger and more memorable things in life.

Take time to define your purpose in life. Becoming financially independent and being able to retire early is not a purpose nor a destination, it is merely a set of tools that allow you to achieve your goals and fulfill the purpose you define.

Everyone will have a unique set of goals and purpose, but some common concepts are:

- Being able to leave an inheritance to your family
- Providing for your family if you unexpectedly pass away
- Paying for your children's or grandchildren's college education
- Traveling the world
- Giving and helping those in need
- Enjoying a stress-free retirement
- Retiring early enough to enjoy your earnings
- Owning a yacht, sports car or beachfront property

Why do you want to achieve financial independence and early retirement?

What do you need to modify in your life to make it possible?

Balance

On one end of the financial spectrum there are spenders. These people get joy out of consumption and live their lives in the moment, often with complete disregard for the future and what consequences their actions will have decades from now. Spenders are more likely to live paycheck to paycheck and find themselves unable to retire, often relying on government assistance and others to care for their basic needs when they become elderly.

On the opposite end you have savers, these people are constantly planning, considering the future, and are so focused on the end goal that life often passes them by without realizing it. Many are able to retire early but are unwilling to since there is always one more financial milestone to achieve. When they finally do get around to retiring, they often don't have the energy left to do the things they always dreamed of doing with the money they worked so hard to earn.

It's critical to find a balance between the two extremes. Small sacrifices early in life will allow you to invest and grow enough wealth to become financially independent, giving you the freedom to retire when you want and live the lifestyle you've always dreamed.

Many years ago, my wife and I took a trip to Jamaica to celebrate our anniversary. One evening, as we sat at the beachside bar watching a beautiful beach sunset, I overheard two businessmen — a tractor salesman from North Dakota and a department manager at a bank in New York City — bragging about their wealth. They were discussing their lucrative careers, the sizes of their homes, and the various sports cars they owned. Finally, one of the gentlemen turned to the bartender, a local Jamaican resident, and said:

"What about you? Do you ever dream of moving to America?"

The bartender laughed and said:

"You American's may have watches, but Jamaicans, we have the time."

For most at the bar, it was merely a whimsical remark that was quickly forgotten. Maybe it was one too many Red Stripes, but that moment was very profound. For me, it was a glimpse into a culture that values freedom and life experiences over physical belongings and the realization that wealth only brings value to your life if you have the time and ability to use it. I have since revised my picture of the American Dream to be a balance of sufficient resources to be financially independent and time to enjoy it. I encourage you to do the same.

What Really Matters

For most people, financial independence will unquestionably contribute to your overall sense of well-being but is not a replacement for close and meaningful connections with the people in your life that you love the most. People who become hyper-obsessed with the acquisition of wealth may struggle with personal relationships as they are unable or unwilling to spend the time necessary to maintain healthy relationships. All of the wealth in the world won't buy you happiness (as the Beatles say, "Money can't buy me love.").

Likewise, a complete disregard for finances can have just as devastating consequences, with effects that are not limited to just our lives. The decisions we make every day have an impact on our community and those closest to us; poor money handling skills can create unnecessary stress on extended family and friends. Whether you like it or not, money is an essential part of our modern economy. In general, the more you the easier life will be. Availability of money, or lack thereof, dictates the quality of food you can afford (fresh fruit and vegetables are more expensive than cheap and unhealthy processed food), the schools your children attend, how often you are able to take vacations, and how long you will have to work before retiring, if at all.

Over 90% of Americans will get married at some point in their lives and is an important part of our culture. Statistically, those who are married live longer, are healthier, happier, and earn more money. How someone chooses to handle their personal finances can either be a blessing or a curse to their marriage. When couples hide expenses, disagree on how to spend money, and what their long-term goals are, it can drive a wedge between them. Couples that learn to handle money properly develop trust, improve their communication skills, and will be able to achieve their goals faster by working together as a team. Married couple are generally more financially successful than singles, not because financially successful people get married, but because marriage helps partners make better financial decisions. A healthy marriage promotes financial success, so it comes as no surprise that 86% of millionaires are married.

You only get one opportunity to walk this planet and you don't want to spend it as a slave to debt, but it's important to not get so caught up in chasing your financial goals that you miss all the joy in life. The goal of this book is not to make you a wealth creating machine, but instead to find a balance between acquiring the wealth needed to be financially independent and doing so early enough to enjoy it.

PAST & PRESENT

"We make ourselves rich by making our wants few."
—Henry David Thoreau

Past

My parents were born and raised in a rural farming community located in northwest Ohio. Married at 18, they rented their first home, a tiny single bedroom farm house with a single cast iron stove for heat. Despite their humble beginnings, they were never afraid to dream big. They studied at the local community college and earned degrees in engineering and accounting, while working full time and raising a family. As their three children grew, so did their goals. After years of saving, they began the construction of their first home. With just three bedrooms and two, bathrooms it was far from a mansion but more than adequate for raising a small family. Now retired, they are reaping the rewards of their financial prudence and decades of diligent investing, allowing them to enjoy the beautiful white sandy beaches and stunning sunsets from the comfort of their beachfront condo in southern Florida.

My grandparents have similar life stories, they started with nothing at a young age but were no strangers to hard work and were smart with their money. They built their own homes, owned only one car through most of their life, and worked multiple jobs all while raising large families. Both of my grandfathers worked long, hard hours in an automotive factory, only to come home and work until the early hours of the morning planting crops on the family farm or building custom wood cabinets in a garage workshop. They grew gardens, cooked meals from scratch, canned extra produce, and lived a lifestyle well within their means. Like my parents, their frugal lifestyle combined with hard work, diligent saving, and investing over a period of decades allowed them to retire wealthy, travel, and spend time with family.

Present

Since the last recession, I routinely hear people gripe that the American Dream is no longer obtainable. Stagnant wages, high home prices, and day-to-day living expenses have become overwhelming for some. We place the blame for our inability to obtain our dreams on banks too big to fail, greedy Wall Street corporations, and corrupt Washington politicians. While some of this may be true, we often overlook how different our standard of living is compared to that of previous generations. Our parents and grandparents didn't have the luxury of multiple vehicles, personal computers, cell phones, cable TV, high speed internet, or other monthly subscriptions such as gym memberships, Netflix or Hulu. They also weren't saddled with the high cost of obtaining the latest and greatest technology or maintaining the monthly subscriptions required to keep these devices operational. There is no question that sophisticated technology has enhanced our lives, making daily activities more convenient and entertaining, but at what cost?

The American Dream has become a lifestyle of instant gratification and excess spending. We no longer think through and save for large purchases. Instead, we impulse shop online using our credit cards to buy items we don't need with money we don't have. We don't have money for the big screen TV we just bought, but we've got until the end of the month to worry about it. If we don't have the money by then we'll just let it ride for a couple months. Sure, it will gain interest, but who cares? There's plenty of time to worry about that in the future!

Today, more young adults attend college than ever before in our nation's history, partially due to the easy access of student loans. Previous generations would have had to work full-time while attending school part-time to pay their way. Easy access to loans helps students graduate faster by allowing them to focus on their academics, and it opens the door to education for millions of Americans who used to not be able to afford it. It also saddles young adults with tens or even hundreds of thousands of dollars of student loan debt. That's a worthwhile investment if you're planning to become a doctor or other high paying professional career, but for most graduates with lower paying careers it has potential to be a catastrophic financial disaster that will take decades to recover.

Additionally, far too many twenty-somethings fall into the trap of trying to achieve a standard of living equal to that of their parents. Attempting to emulate one's parents is certainly a worthwhile goal; only they desire to live that lifestyle now and disregard the decades of hard work and countless sacrifices their parents made that allow them to enjoy a high standard of living.

Have you ever purchased a luxury item that you later regretted?

Luxury items are the reward of financial success and are intended to be enjoyed by those with two commas in their net worth. People not of the upper echelon can end up resenting the luxury items they purchase because they become a financial burden. At some point, our nation decided that short-term pain was not worth long-term gain, instead opting for instant gratification financed by mountains of debt to enjoy a lifestyle we can't realistically afford.

Retire Early, Retire Rich

DEBT

"Gold is the money of kings, silver is the money of gentlemen, barter is the money of peasants – but debt is the money of slaves."

—Norman Franz

Money may not be able to buy you happiness, but the lack of it can make your life miserable. When you borrow money, you give up control over a portion of your time and income. Not only do you have to pay of the original loan amount, you now must work extra to pay off the accumulated interest. For many, debt is equivalent to modern day slavery, forcing them to work for those who have learned how to master their money. There's always a tomorrow for which to work, but a looming cloud of debt makes the future seem uncertain, frightening, and even hopeless.

Most people react to debt by trying to earn their way out of foolish financial decisions. They believe if they can just get a raise, bonus, higher paying job, or pick up a few extra hours of overtime that they will be able to clean up the mess they created. But very few people maintain their current standard of living when their income increases. For most Americans, raises are followed by celebratory vacations, new car purchases, or big screen TVs. This financial phenomenon is so common that financial advisors refer to it as "lifestyle creep".

Unfortunately, lifestyle creep is most common among those approaching retirement age. Not only does it prevent them from caching necessary retirement savings, but they develop a taste for a lavish lifestyle that their retirement accounts are unable to support. Items once considered luxuries when they were younger are now considered normal and necessary aspects of everyday life. A fancy dinner at a steak house used to be a once a year event for a birthday or anniversary, but with subsequent pay raises, it becomes the regular Friday night dinner, where the servers know your name. To grow wealth at a rate necessary to achieve financial independence and early retirement, one must strive to maintain an efficient lifestyle even in the face of raises and career advancements. Continuing to live like a poor college kid even long after graduation is a sure-fire path towards early retirement.

Credit Card Debt

Almost all forms of debt are terrible for your finances, but credit card debt should be avoided like the plague. The average American with credit card debt carries a balance of over $16,000. With an Annual Percentage Rate (APR) of 20% or greater, credit card debt can easily spiral out of control. When starting your journey to financial freedom high interest credit card debt should be tackled first.

Once the credit cards are paid off, it is important to avoid future overuse. For some this may mean putting them in a safe spot in your home (instead of your wallet or purse), while others go as far as freezing credit cards (literally) in a block of ice, that way they are there if you really need them but makes impulse shopping very difficult. For those who struggle with debt, your best option would be to cut up and cancel all your credit cards.

Debit cards offer the same function and flexibility as credit cards, only they draw directly from your checking account. Just be sure to keep an eye on your account balance so you don't get hit with an overdraft penalty.

Vehicles

Personal vehicles are one of the largest sources of debt and reoccurring monthly payments for most American middle-class families. According to a 2017 Kelly Blue Book study, the average new car purchase price is $36,113 and we replace our vehicle approximately every five years. Unfortunately, vehicles are not known for their ability to hold value. A new car will lose approximately 10% of its value the moment it is driven off the dealer's lot. That means the ink from your signature hasn't even dried and you've already lost approximately $3,611. After the first year of ownership your vehicle will have lost an additional 10% and by year five it will have lost over 60% of its original value.

I learned firsthand of this rapid depreciation of value, when my vehicle was rear-ended at a stop light. Due to excessive damage (the rear passenger seats were now in the trunk), the insurance company declared the vehicle totaled and wrote me a check for the value of the car. Only the check was less than the remaining debt owed. This is an increasingly common problem among new car sales, especially with the introduction of six, seven, and even eight-year loan periods. Longer loan periods result in more interest and less principal being paid off in the earlier years of the loan, creating a large gap between the actual value of the car and the remaining loan amount.

To address this issue automobile manufacturers, offer "gap insurance" to cover the difference between the remaining loan amount and the actual value of the vehicle. For an additional charge, of course.

Until you have amassed a substantial net worth it is recommended to avoid buying new cars. Instead, save up and pay in full for a quality used vehicle. This lets the original owner eat the depreciation in value and allows you to save thousands of dollars each year. This goes against cultural norms, but when broke is the norm, sometimes it's best not to follow the herd.

Debt Consolidation

This is the process of taking out a personal loan through a bank or credit union to pay off your outstanding debt. You will end up with a single loan, typically with lower monthly payments. For those who had missed payments, it also stops the creditors from harassing you.

However, debt consolidation should always be carefully considered as there are disadvantages hidden in the numbers. Let's look at an example:

Imagine you have two auto loans that are both $400 per month over a four-year period and a personal loan that is $200 per month over two-years, for a total payment of $1,000 per month. After consolidating into a single loan, your payment drops to $500 per month for 5 years. That's wonderful! You're saving $500 a month...right?

No, not really. Your original loans would have been $24,000 over a four-year period, but the debt consolidation loan will cost you $30,000 over a five-year period. The original set of loans would have gotten you out of debt one year earlier and saved you $6,000.

Debt consolidation is not a magic pill that will solve all your financial problems; it's impossible to pay off debt by taking out more debt. If you don't change your spending habits and address the reasons for why you were in debt in the first place, you're just rearranging deck chairs on the Titanic. Everything looks neat and organized, but you're still sinking.

Student Loans
Student loan debt is a $1.5 trillion crisis (and growing) that affects more than 44 million borrowers in the U.S. The average student has a shocking $37,172 in student loan debt. While college has prepared millions of Americans for more advanced and ever-changing career fields, it has also saddled them with mountains of debt. While small in comparison to other debts (ex: auto loans or home mortgages), the timing at the beginning of one's career, is what arguably makes student loans more financially devastating. Instead of maxing out a 401(k) and taking advantage of compound interest, young employees are forced to divert funds away from saving and investing in order to pay down debt.

Many young adults have mistakenly followed bad advice, being told to keep their student loans as they can be forgiven or that a proposed law, if passed, or politician, if elected will supposedly be able to wash away their financial sins.

A few of the more common student loan forgiveness plans are:

- **Public Service Loan Forgiveness** – Employees, who work full time for the government, non-profit organizations, or in the public sector, may qualify for the Public Service Loan Forgiveness Program. This plan will repay 100% of the remaining loan balance after 20 or 25 years of regular loan payments.

- **Income Based Repayment Plan (IBR)** – This program allows borrowers with loans taken out after July 1, 2014, who are suffering from financial hardship, to use a non-standard payment plan that is designed to not exceed 10% of their discretionary income for a 20-year period.

- **Teacher Loan Forgiveness** – Available to teachers who work a minimum of five years in low income areas. This plan pays up to $17,500 of remaining student loan debt for special education, math, and science teachers. All other teachers can receive up to $5,000.

- **Perkins Loan Cancellation** – Graduates who took out Perkins Loans can cancel a percentage of their Perkins student loan debt each year over a five-year period.

The biggest flaw of the student loan forgiveness programs is that by time the borrower qualifies to have their loans forgiven, they will have made regular payments on the loan for 10 to 20-years, at which point there will be little or no remaining balance to be forgiven.

If you are in a tight financial situation or have a career that allows you to qualify for a loan forgiveness program, be sure to take advantage of the options out there to help you; however, the best strategy for dealing with student loans is to avoid them in the first place. If loans are necessary, every effort should be made to reduce the amount of money borrowed. Most importantly, they should be treated as a top priority and paid off as soon as possible, allowing you to free up funds for investing.

Most financial advisors agree that a student should never take out loans greater than their anticipated starting salary. For example, a student studying to be a school teacher should not take out loans greater than $30,000, an engineer may be able to afford loans up to about $50,000, and a pharmacist or other medical professional should have little trouble repaying student loans in excess of $100,000. Every student will need to investigate reasonable loan amounts for themselves, but the ideal amount is always the smallest possible.

In addition to the amount of the loans, it is important to vet loan sources. There are a myriad of options, both private and governmental, which offer varying interest rates and repayment terms. It is vitally important to understand the terms and conditions of all the student loan options available before making a final decision.

CUTTING EXPENSES

"There are thousands and thousands of people out there, leading lives of quiet, screaming desperation, where they work long, hard hours at jobs they hate to enable them to buy things they don't need to impress people they don't like."
—Nigel Marsh

Most people spend thousands or even tens of thousands of dollars on unnecessary expenses each year. Even small purchases, if frequent enough, will hinder your ability save and invest without you even realizing it. For most, these hidden expenses come in the form of a morning routine of stopping at a favorite local coffee shop to pick up an overpriced latte and bagel or buying snacks out of vending machines at work that are three to four times as expensive as in the grocery store.

The recommendations listed in this chapter are all actions you can take right now to improve your financial situation. They require no education, training or risk, and require far less effort than would be needed to increase your income by an equivalent dollar amount.

Cutting expenses is not about living an extremely frugal, hermit-like life style, void of belonging or entertainment. It's about identifying your priorities and eliminating wasteful sources of spending that are robbing you of long-term wealth, while still maintaining a comfortable and enjoyable standard of living.

Create a Budget

Creating a budget is an essential tool for identifying sources of wasteful spending and planning your monthly expenses. A simple hand-written budget is a great way to start and an excellent ice breaker when talking with a spouse or partner who may be reluctant to discuss finances. Microsoft Excel can be used to create a more detailed budget and will allow you to easily customize your monthly budget. There are also numerous free budgeting tools available online or on your mobile device such as Mint.com, PersonalCapital.com, and Betterment.com. These apps can be directly linked to credit cards, savings, checking, and investment accounts to provide a complete up to date view of your current financial situation and track spending by category from month-to-month. These will help you realize trends and easily identify wasteful spending. They can even be used to set reminders to make sure credit cards and bills are paid on time or alert you of suspicious or high dollar purchases.

Retail Therapy

According to Huffington Post, one in three Americans shop to reduce stress. Unfortunately, this creates a disastrous perpetual financial and emotional cycle which runs up credit card debt, causes additional stress, which in turn causes one to go buy more stuff.

If you are a shopaholic, be sure to leave your credit card at home and only bring the exact amount of cash you need for the purchase when you go to the store. If you shop for entertainment, try to find a different source of entertainment. Take a walk in the park, ride a bike, pick up a new hobby, anything that keeps you out of a store. A recovering alcoholic knows to stay out of a bar, likewise a shopaholic should avoid the mall.

Stop Dining Out

According to a 2015 Bureau of Labor Statistics, the average American household spends $3,008 a year eating out. Meals can be cooked at home for as little as 20% of the cost of dining out, likely less if you consider the hidden costs such as tipping, transportation to the restaurant, and paying for parking. If you regularly eat out for lunch, packing leftovers from dinner the night before can save you thousands of dollars and countless calories each year.

If you aren't willing to completely stop eating out, try just ordering a water to drink. Restaurant drinks carry some of the highest markups on the menu. The average restaurant price for a soda is $2.00, yet it only costs them $0.15 per drink. At that price, you would have to drink 14 sodas to get your money's worth.

Planning Meals

To fully take advantage of the reduced cost of cooking at home, you should plan the majority of your meals in advance. Create a menu and take inventory of the food on hand before going to the grocery store. This will allow you to shop for the best deals, avoid over purchasing common items, and helps you reduce hectic last-minute trips which consume valuable free time and create unnecessary stress. Picking up a gallon of milk at 6 p.m. during the middle of the week is about as relaxing as navigating a New York City subway during rush-hour.

When planning meals, try to overlap as many ingredients as possible; leftover rice from stir fry on Monday can be used on Taco Tuesdays. Once removed from the package a block of cheese can go bad fast, so use it for homemade mac and cheese one day and make grilled cheese later in the week. Meal planning is a great way to create a menu based on available coupons and weekly store specials. Most major grocery store chains offer digital coupon apps, but the newspaper and a pair of scissors work just as well as it did before the internet was invented. Many areas in and surrounding larger cities have distributions of coupon magazines which are a free or low-cost alternative to a newspaper subscription. Coordinating ingredients, cutting coupons, and planning your meals around in-store specials can easily save you 30-40% on grocery bills. Depending on the size of your family this could be anywhere from a few hundred to a few thousands in savings each year.

Cutting Cable

Americans spend a staggering five hours a day watching television. With the average cable bill more than $100 a month, plus an additional $50 for high speed internet, it is one of our largest monthly expenses, with rates increasing annually. By canceling my cable and reducing the internet to the slowest speed my bill went from $150 to $20! With the purchase of an inexpensive over-the-air HD TV antenna, you will have access to dozens of _free_ high definition channels. I'm able to receive over 60 channels, but the selection of channels available will vary based on your location. If you desire the convenient features of cable TV, consider a Channel Master DVR, a subscription _free_ over the air DVR that allows you to record your favorite shows, pause live TV, and provides an easy to navigate TV guide.

For those that are not quite ready to give up their favorite cable shows, Sling TV is a great way to cut the cost of your subscription without feeling like much of a sacrifice. This à la carte TV service allows to pick individual channels from various popular categories such as sports, news, and movies that are normally only included in the highest dollar cable TV packages. This internet TV service still requires a monthly internet subscription.

Cell Phones

Nearly half of all smartphone users replace their device every two years. With the cost of the latest phones pushing $1000, delaying a new purchase, especially if your current phone is fully paid for, is an easy way to save money. Another strategy is to purchase older discontinued or refurbished models, both of which will be a fraction of the price of the latest-and-greatest models.

If possible, take advantage of family and group discount plans which allow you to share the base cost of the plan with multiple users. Just be sure you know and trust the person in charge of the account; if the person paying the bill is notorious for missing payments or routinely using more than their portion of a shared data plan, it can create a lot of frustration.

Negotiate Lower Subscription Rates

Subscription memberships and other reoccurring expenses are a constant drain on your wealth. Unused or unneeded memberships should always be canceled, but it is often easier said than done. Many membership business models depend on the majority of their customers regularly paying but rarely utilizing the services offered. The most notable example is gym memberships, where new members sign up to drop a few pounds for a New Year's resolution, quickly lose interest but never bother to cancel their membership. Gyms are also notoriously aggressive, often requiring their members to provide bank account information rather than a credit card. All credit cards are issued with expiration dates, which prevent the gym from charging monthly fees once a card has expired. By tapping directly into your bank account, the only way they will stop receiving funds is if the member physically comes to the gym, has the unpleasant conversation, and fills out the mountain of paperwork necessary to cancel the membership. Sadly, some people would rather keep paying for an unused membership than deal with the hassle of canceling, don't be that person.

A few examples of common subscription services are:

- Netflix
- Hulu
- Amazon Prime
- Cloud and online digital media storage
- Website memberships
- Upgraded video game content
- VIP access
- Website hosting
- Cell phones
- Landline phones
- Cable TV
- Internet

- Satellite radio
- Home security system
- Magazines
- "Item" of the month clubs
- Meal services (Blue Apron, Hello Fresh)
- Landscaping services
- Gym memberships
- Lessons (piano, swimming, dancing, horse riding, etc...)

If you are unable or unwilling to live without a service requiring a monthly expense, it doesn't mean you have to pay full price. The art of negotiating can be used to reduce the cost of monthly subscriptions by taking advantage of promotional deals and using some of the same methods they use to lock in new customers against them to lower your rates.

When it comes to negotiating, knowledge is power. You will need to research the prices, terms, and packages your current service provider and its competitors are offering in your area. This information will provide you with bargaining power and will let you know ahead of time how much of a discount is reasonable. If they can offer a low price to attract new customers, they are more than likely willing to offer it to existing customers to prevent them from canceling services or switching to a competitor. It's a good idea to have paper and pencil on hand to take notes during the conversation. You'll want to document the name of the person you spoke with, when the conversation took place, and the information they provided you (terms and condition of the deal agreed upon). It may seem overwhelming at first, but it can be broken down into three simple steps:

- **Research** – Start by signing into your account or reviewing your latest statement you received in the mail. Before making the phone call, take the time to write a list of the key pieces of information about the company, their competitors, and what options are available. At a minimum, this information should include the following:

   I.   Your account number
   II. How long you have been a loyal customer
   III. Promotional deals they are offering
   IV. Promotional deals their competitors are offering
   V.   Different subscription levels
   VI. Any student or senior citizen discounts you qualify for

- **Negotiate** – Start your conversation by being as friendly as possible. Customer services representatives deal with angry customers all day long, so avoid raising your voice or making harsh demands. If you can make a personal connection and get them to like you and sympathize with your situation, they will be more likely to help you. From personal experience, I've found calling in the morning, usually about an hour after the company opens, yields the best results. By this point in the day, most employees will have had their morning coffee, assuring they are awake and alert, but not having been at work long enough to have dealt with multiple upset customers. If you end up with someone who is frustrated and uncooperative, just hang up and try again later. Most call centers have dozens of employees answering the phones, eventually you will find someone willing to negotiate.

Let the representative know you are a loyal customer and never miss payments but are having troubling keeping up with your bill or are unhappy with your existing service and are considering canceling. Ask to be transferred to the cancellation department, where representatives have more freedom to negotiate and are trained to do whatever it takes to retain existing customers. Keep your initial request simple. Try saying something like:

"I have been using your services for many years but am unable to afford my monthly bill anymore and am thinking about canceling my service. What can you do to help me out?"

If possible, try to let the customer service representative do most of the talking by asking open ended questions such as:

"What can you do to reduce my monthly bill?"
"What can you do to get me a cheaper plan?"
"What promotional deals are you offering right now?"

They may be authorized to offer deals that are not advertised to the general public. Most companies will not risk losing a long-term customer over a few dollars, even if that means offering a temporary discount or free upgraded services.

If they still won't budge, let them know what deals their competitors are offering to attract new customers. Typically, they will be able match the deal or offer a deal of equal or greater value.

Typically, promotional deals are not permanent changes to your bill, and will only last for a few months to a year. After the deal expires your rates will return to normal. It's important to note that they will begin charging you for any free services they may have added to your deal. For example, your cable provider may offer you a free movie channel for six-months, but once the deal expires, they will start charging you each month for the extra channel, so be sure to call and cancel any additional services before they are added to your bill. The company is gambling that you will either forget to cancel the service or get used to the extra service and keep paying.

- **Follow Up** – The final step is to check your account online or review your next mailed statement to confirm all the agreed upon changes were made. Some companies will process the changes immediately, while others may wait for the next billing period. Remember, customer service representatives handle hundreds of calls every day. Just because they say the changes were made doesn't mean they actually were. Your request may not have been properly processed or rejected by another internal department. If the changes don't match the agreed upon terms, you will need to repeat the negotiation process.

If after multiple attempts you are unable to negotiate a better deal, don't be afraid to cancel your service. If you did your research, you will already know about a better offer you can go with instead.

Extended Warranties

While not a legal requirement, most products come with a manufacturer's warranty, which covers any defects from the manufacturing process. An extended warranty is an additional warranty plan sold to customers as an add-on, typically at the register. With pages of fine print, and a dozen people in the checkout line, an extended warranty sounds like a good idea at the time, but most people have little knowledge of what it does (or doesn't) cover. The truth is most plans have high deductibles, may not cover accidental damage, and often exclude key mechanical and electronic components.

One popular cellular network offers an extended warranty on their cell phones for $10 per month plus a $200 deductible. Assuming your phone breaks after two years, it would cost you a total of $440 to replace it using the warranty plan. For that price, you could easily pay out of pocket to replace your broken phone. After two years it has likely been replaced by several newer generations, which would allow you to replace it for a fraction of its original purchase price. If you're worried about damaging your phone, purchasing a quality name brand protective case is likely more valuable than any cell phone warranty plan.

Extended warranties are basically insurance for consumer products. As a general rule, insurance should only be purchased to cover the cost of catastrophic events to highly valuable items you can't afford out of pocket to replace, such as a vehicle, home or major medical expense. If you have to purchase insurance for a DVD player because you are unable to replace it if it breaks, you should probably rethink the purchase in the first place.

Take a "Staycation"

According to American Express, the average cost for a family vacation is $4,580. We all need time off from our hectic schedules to rest and rejuvenate, but it doesn't have to cost thousands of dollars. Take advantage of inexpensive activities like visiting local parks, going camping in your backyard, turning your bathroom into a spa, hosting a board game tournament, cooking a tropical themed dinner or decorating your home like your favorite relaxing destination. Keep in mind that some vacations can be physically and mentally exhausting. Sometimes a few days at home can be more relaxing than taking a trip to a theme park on the other side of the country.

Cutting Your Own Hair

Shortly after getting married, my wife decided that her newly acquired last name (Barber) meant she was qualified to cut my hair. I was reluctant at first, but the thought of saving $20 every two weeks was enough of an incentive for me to give it a try. After watching a few videos online and buying a $15 hair trimmer, she was a pro! Cutting my hair at home means I don't have to sit at a busy barber shop on Saturday mornings for over an hour waiting in line for my turn to get my hair cut and it saves us over $500 a year!

Buy in Bulk

Shopping in bulk at wholesale/club stores like Costco and Sam's Club can add up to thousands of dollars of savings per year, especially for those with large families. Just be sure to only purchase items you frequently use and compare prices to your regular grocery store. Just because something is being sold in a bulk package doesn't necessarily mean it is cheaper per ounce. Most club stores require a paid membership but the savings from your first trip combined with the coupons they offer when you sign up will likely more than cover the cost. Also, keep an eye out for membership deals on Groupon type websites.

Cash is King

When you purchase an item with a credit or debit card, the store has to pay the credit card company a fee anywhere from 3-5%. You can use this knowledge to your advantage to get discounts on larger value items. For example, I saved 3% when I purchased my wife's engagement ring with cash. When my air conditioning unit needed replaced they lowered the bill from $4,200 to $4,000 when I offered to write a check instead of using a credit card. Not all businesses are able or willing to offer a cash discount, but it doesn't hurt to ask.

Raising Kids

Raising kids doesn't have to be as financially devastating as some make it out to be. Many parents claim they struggle financially because raising children is so expensive, but the reality is most would likely be in the same financial shape even if they had no kids. The money they spend raising children would instead go towards a bigger home, nicer vacation, newer TV, or a bass boat.

While many of the expenses of raising children are non-negotiable, such as healthcare or making sure they have access to nutritious meals, there are areas in which parents can sway from the traditional methods to save money and help better their children's lives at the same time.

Retire Early, Retire Rich

A 2017 study performed by WorldAtlas.com, determined that Americans are the second highest consumers of children's toys, spending on average $371 per child each year, or $6,678 by time they are adults. When surveyed, children indicated that nearly two-thirds of their toys were unwanted, unused, or still sealed in original packaging. Every parent has been through that disheartening moment when they watch their child unwrapped an expensive toy, open the box, toss the $100+ toy aside and proceed to play with the free cardboard box the toy came in.

Think back to your childhood, what do you remember?

My childhood memories are of experiences spent with my family, not colorful plastic toys, which are likely at the bottom of a landfill by now. Sure, the presents were nice, but what made holidays and birthdays so memorable was the time spend with my family. When you do buy toys, invest in the ones that have lots of replay value and will last a lifetime. For example, I still play with the LEGO bricks I got as a child over 25 years ago, as will my children and grandchildren. My nephews play with the same Lincoln Logs that my parents got when they were kids.

As children get older they will want to make their own purchases and have more freedom with how they spend their money. At some point they will (or already have) come to you asking for money. Fight the urge to give them an allowance. While it does teach them to budget and keep their spending within their weekly/monthly limit, it does a poor job teaching them where money comes from. Instead, pay them based on performance. An allowance may cause young adults to develop an entitlement mentality in which they are rewarded for simply existing, whereas performance-based pay teaches them they only receive payment when tasks are completed. Some parents feel bad making their kids pay for their own toys and expenses, but it teaches them the value of money, how to properly handle it, and critical negotiating skills they will be able to use as adults. Not only will it cause them to spend less money, but they will take much better care of the items they buy. The sooner they realize the value of a dollar, the better off they will be as adults, and you are teaching them life lessons that most young adults don't experience for the first time until they are in their mid-20's or older.

When planning family activities, trips to amusement parks, movies, and sporting events can be extremely costly activities, especially for large families. Instead, focus on fun, healthy activities with little or no cost that will teach them valuable life skills. Here are a few inexpensive activities the entire family can enjoy:

- Apple picking
- Baking
- Building paper airplanes
- Building houses out of cardboard boxes
- Camping
- Finger painting
- Flying kites
- Going to a playground/park
- Going to the beach
- Going to the library
- Hiking
- Having a picnic
- Running a lemonade stand
- Playing board games
- Playing sports
- Putting up holiday decoration
- Recording home videos
- Riding bikes
- Telling ghost stories
- Volunteering
- Watching movies at home

Never Pay Retail

Whenever you're planning a purchase, be sure to check online before buying it in the store at full price. You can often find the identical product you are looking for on eBay or Amazon for less than retail store prices. Many stores, such as Target and Walmart, will price match online stores. Additionally, online shopping has the added benefit of saving you time, gas, and in some states, you aren't required to pay sales tax. For larger items, check Craigslist, thrift stores, or auctions where you can buy new or gently used clothing, furniture, toys and much more for pennies on the dollar.

If possible, buy items at the end of the season. Summer clothes end up on the discount racks in the fall and winter clothes get marked down in the spring. The best time to buy 4th of July decorations is July 5th. Halloween candy is usually 50-75% off on November 1st and can have an expiration date of several years. Use this tip to cut down on the cost of next year's treats or give double the amount to those goblins and ghouls. Be sure to hide the candy well enough to avoid the temptation of breaking into the bags mid-year, but not well enough that you forget where you put it. For me, putting up Christmas lights and decorations are some of my favorite things about the holiday. Despite this, I may have just a little Scrooge in me: the prices of decorations are cringe worthy. I take note of what lights need replaced, what I would like for next year, and make my purchases the week after Christmas to get discounts as high as 70-90%.

Black Friday is one method of cutting costs by which some people swear by, but from personal experience, I don't think it's worth the headache. Black Friday pushes hyper-consumerism, highlighting greedy and compulsive behavior, and in some rare cases even sparks violence (ironically on a day intended for families to give thanks and blessing for what they have). Setting aside the negative social aspects, Black Friday is rarely the financial bargain people hope it to be. Retailers often markup prices in the weeks leading up to Black Friday just so they can offer what appear to be remarkable sales. They also lure thousands of shoppers into their stores with shady marketing tactics and the false hopes that they will be able to buy the $1,000 flat screen TV for $300. They know very well there might only be 3-4 big ticket items in each store, nowhere near enough to meet the actual demand for these items. Manufacturers are not ignorant of this – some actually produce products that look the part but have less or lower quality features. Be certain of your purchase on Black Friday! Retailers are willing to take a loss on a few high dollar items because they know once you've waited for hours in the freezing cold, you will not go home empty handed, even if it means buying something you didn't intend.

Gift Giving Guilt

We live in a culture full of advertising and marketing that tells us the only way to let someone know how much we care about them is to spend money, preferably in large amounts, on cheaply manufactured disposable goods that you will have to buy again in the near future. Nothing says 'I love you' like a toaster that burns and image of your face directly onto the toast (because the last thing I want to see in the morning is my portrait in bread).

But the madness doesn't stop there, if you're going to give someone cash, you have to buy a $5 card to put it in. Instead, make a card from construction paper or print a free one online.

The average American spends over $935 each year at Christmas, and in exchange they receive a closet full of decorative socks, itchy sweaters, candles, and countless other items they would never buy for themselves. The few days after Christmas are often the busiest days of the years for returns as millions of people flock to stores with unwanted gifts.

Buying an excessive number of gifts will not bring happiness or respect from others, and the dollar amount you spend does not directly translate into how much you care. The best way to break this cycle is through communication. As families grow, it's a great idea to have an open discussion on what the holiday season and those special events really mean to everyone. Often people are reluctant to bring up the topic of reducing gift giving as they're afraid people will view them as cheap. You might be surprised to find out others are thinking the exact same thing and are relieved someone finally brought it up. Even small limits per person can add up to hundreds of dollars when you are buying gifts for extended family. Reducing what you buy for others not only lightens the load on your pocketbook, but it helps reduce those stressful visits to the mall and clutter in your home.

Secret Santa or a White Elephant gift exchanges are great ways to keep the tradition of generosity and gift giving alive, while not overwhelming people with unwanted gifts and burdening them with the expense of having to buy excessive presents. Thanksgiving is a great time to bring up the idea of a gift exchange and selecting names from a hat for your Secret Santa can become a part of your family's holiday tradition.

Don't be afraid to go homemade. Some of the best gifts I've ever received were inexpensive and came from the heart, such as a framed photos and unique personalized items. Some of my wife's favorite gifts I've given her over the years are homemade cards. I'm by no means an artist, but my cards, made of folded construction paper and crudely drawn stick figures were thoughtful (and hilariously pathetic at times) because of the message it conveyed. It's a one of a kind gift you can't buy in a store and something you can't put a price tag on.

Gift giving guilt is not exclusive to the holiday season; it can be for a graduation, anniversary, or your goldfish's third birthday. Whatever the occasion, the gifts you give (if any) should focus on the meaning of the special occasion, not the dollar amount.

INCOME

"You must gain control over your money or the lack of it will forever control you."
—Dave Ramsey

Increasing the income from your career is probably the most obvious way to build wealth and allow for early retirement, but before you storm into your boss' office demanding a raise, you must first be able to show how you are bringing additional value to the company. This could include showing an increase in your sales numbers, working extra uncompensated hours to accommodate a demanding client, or completing obligations not outlined in the original job description, such as a significant increase in travel time or attending work related meetings or events outside of regular business hours.

Training and education is another way of increasing your income. You will often earn more with a master's, than a bachelor's, or associate's degree. Many companies even offer compensation to cover the cost of higher education. Talk with your boss or a representative in human resources to find out how you can take advantage of all the benefits that are available. You can also seek out additional skills, such as safety training, word processing, management training, and other courses to help increase your value to your employer.

Be sure to consider the timing when you meet with your boss to ask for a raise or bonus. The best time is typically a month or two before your annual review. This allows your employer to review your request and process any paper work prior to your formal meeting. Cost of living increases and raises are often given out during annual reviews, so it's easy for your manager to provide your raise without additional paperwork, supervisor approval, or taking up his/her valuable time to meet with you an additional time regarding your pay increase.

Sometimes even the most dedicated and hardworking employees will find themselves in a rut. Many factors can contribute to this including repetitious tasks or a lack of opportunities to advance within the company. Changing jobs or entire career paths can be a very stressful decision but may be required for you to advance your career and typically results in an increase in pay and better opportunities for growth within your desired career path. The key to making a successful move is not to be desperate. Don't wait until you've been laid off to decide to make that big career change. It's much more advantageous to explore options while still collecting a paycheck. Changing jobs when you are free from fear is important because you are able to negotiate and only accept a new position when the terms are in your favor. Desperate people are often forced take the first job offer they get, no matter how unfavorable it is because there are mouths to feed and the mortgage is due.

Most people do fine networking externally but completely overlook networking internally within their company. This is especially true for large corporations with hundreds or thousands of employees and multiple offices. You must learn to sell yourself to other co-workers and managers. As you build a solid reputation of being trustworthy and hardworking, you will have no trouble asking for pay raises and will already be on management's radar when they are looking to fill a higher-level position.

Wealthy individuals typically do not earn all their money from one source. They tend to naturally develop and grow a variety of skills and create multiple sources of income, which allows them to increase their wealth faster and have more control over their own financial situation. If 100% of your income comes from XYZ Corporation and they go out of business you have lost all your income and must scramble to find a new job, any job, just to pay the bills. If your job at XYZ is only 75% of your income, you will have more time to react in the event of a job loss. For some, losing their primary income is an opportunity to expand a side business or create a full-time business out of their supplemental income source.

Supplemental Income

Supplemental income can be any compensation earned outside of your regular income. This can include overtime pay, bonuses, and commissions, however, this section will focus on developing multiple sources of income outside of your career. This is important for employees who receive a fixed salary or are not eligible for overtime pay. Diversifying your skills will make you more valuable in the workforce and has the potential to open the door to a more emotionally and financially rewarding career.

When working on the side to earn supplemental income, be sure to market yourself and your business by taking advantage of free advertising. Many online printing companies offer free promotional business cards, which you can hand out to potential customers. Social media is also a free and powerful tool that can reach thousands of people at the click of a button. Tweet about the services you offer, and post pictures on Instagram and Pinterest of the products you have for sale. Creating a small business Facebook page is a free and simple way to let your friends, family, and potential customers know what you've started a business and what value it can bring to them.

If you're looking for some ideas to create supplemental income, consider some of the following:

- Coaching a school sports team
- Refereeing your favorite sport
- Teaching college courses as an adjunct professor
- Delivering pizzas on weekends
- Providing lawn care services (mowing, shoveling snow, and raking leaves)
- Cleaning houses

- Painting houses
- Dog walking
- House sitting
- Baby sitting
- Baking
- Wedding photography
- Managing social media for small businesses
- Designing websites
- Repairing computers
- Repairing cars
- Gardening and canning
- Starting an eBay resale business
- Having a garage sale

Passive Income

Passive income is a reoccurring source of income that requires minimal effort to maintain once the initial setup is complete. The advantage to passive income is that you avoid exchanging your time for money and generate income no matter what you are doing. It doesn't matter if you're out golfing, sleeping, or sitting on the beach with your toes in the sand, you are constantly making money. The initial setup of a source of passive income can be very labor intensive and may require a great deal of capital to get started.

For example, to develop a source of rental income one must make a significant financial investment in real estate, which may also include costly renovations and repairs. But once a renter is in place, your role may be reduced to mowing the lawn and simply collecting the monthly rent. Once you acquire enough units, you will be able to hire workers to manage and maintain the units for you. Other sources of passive income require little or no capital investment but require a great deal of time; for example, writing a book requires no capital but may take months or even years to complete. The following is a list of ideas for generating passive income you might want to consider.

- Purchase rental properties
- Rent out a spare bedroom
- Host a foreign exchange student
- Collect royalties on an invention
- Collect royalties from writing a book
- Create a drop shipping business
- Invest in dividend paying stocks
- Invest in a startup business
- Collect ad revenue from a website or YouTube channel

Monetize Your Hobbies

Hobbies are an important part of our lives. They allow us to meet like-minded people, relieve stress, avoid boredom, and keep us active and youthful, but they can also be very expensive. It's important to not jeopardize your financial well-being by overspending on your hobbies. A rough rule of thumb is not to spend more than 10% of your take home income, but ideally much less. If you ever find yourself hiding the true cost to your hobby from your spouse or others, it's likely an indication that you are overspending.

Below is a list of common expensive hobbies. Are any of your pastimes on this list?

- Aquariums
- Ballroom dancing
- Collecting art
- Collecting cars
- Collecting coins
- Flying
- Gambling
- Golfing
- Horseback riding
- Mountain climbing
- Racing cars

- Sailing
- Scuba diving
- Sky diving
- World traveling

If you're struggling to justify the high cost of one of your favorite hobbies, try turning it into a profitable (or at least cost neutral) side business. If you are into coin collecting, you can likely easily identify a coin's grade, rarity, and value, which allows you to locate good deals and resell coins for a profit. Setting up an eBay account is a fantastic tool for reaching millions of people around the world who share the same interest.

If your favorite hobby is skill-based, such as horseback riding, surfing, or golfing, you can teach lessons to novices. Almost, every hobby has the potential to create additional income. My neighbor loves knitting and began dying her own yarn to cut down on the cost of materials. When fellow knitters heard what she was doing, they asked if she would teach them. Her classes were small and informal at first, but quickly grew, she now hosts her yarn dying and knitting class to over a dozen students every month.

There are hundreds of inexpensive hobbies that have little or no upfront cost to get started. Many can even be used to produce supplemental income or reduce living expenses. Try and replace one of your more expensive hobbies with one from the list below or go online and see what else you can find. The possibilities are endless.

- Astronomy
- Automotive repair
- Baking
- Basketball
- Brewing beer
- Biking
- Board games

- Building computers
- Canning
- Chess
- Cooking
- Disc golf
- Drawing
- Fishing (without a boat)
- Fitness
- Gardening
- Hiking
- Kayaking
- Learning languages
- Meditation
- Music
- Origami
- Painting
- Photography (digital)
- Photo editing
- Reading
- Running
- Soccer
- Tie dye
- Knitting
- Volunteering
- Wine making
- Wood working
- Writing
- Yoga

Retire Early, Retire Rich

SAVING

"It's not how much money you make, but how much money you keep, how hard it works for you, and how many generations you keep it for."
—Robert Kiyosaki

Growing wealth is not about how much you earn, it's about how much you save and invest. Someone earning a modest household income of $50,000, who saves 50% of their income ($25,000) a year will have greater wealth and be able to retire years earlier than a doctor or a lawyer who earns $200,000 but only saves 5% of their income ($10,000). The traditional recommend saving/investing rate throughout history has been around 10-15%. This is fine if you're going the traditional route of a 35+ year career, but if you desire to retire early and retire rich, you must strive to achieve a significantly higher rate of savings: 50% or more is not uncommon among people seeking early retirement. To become wealthy, you need to invest and use compounding interest to grow your wealth, but you can't start if you don't save money first. This seems like a very simple concept, something even a young child could grasp, yet seven out of ten homes live paycheck to paycheck with no ability to cover even the smallest of unexpected expenses. Did you know that 45 million people receive benefits from the Supplemental Nutrition Assistance Program (food stamps)? That's one out of every seven U.S. citizens. If you are part of the middle-class and can afford to pay your bills and put food on the table, don't squander the chance to create wealth that will last your family for generations.

Emergency Fund

Your grandparents might have called it a "rainy day fund", but this emergency fund should contain enough money to cover 3-6 months of expenses. The money should be kept liquid, which means in a checking or savings account, allowing for quick access to cover unexpected costs, such as car repairs, job loss, or medical expenses. Your emergency fund will likely end up being tens of thousands of dollars, so it's important to resist the urge to invest it in stocks or other high interest earning accounts. The problem with stock investments is, they are not liquid and may require weeks or even months to sell your shares to convert to cash. There is also risk that market fluctuations may wipe out a large portion of the value of your investment when you need it the most. The purpose of an emergency fund is to cover large expenses without having to go into debt. While emergency funds don't earn you interest, they do keep you from paying it.

Certificates of Deposits

A certificate of deposit (CD) is a method of saving where banks and credit unions sell saving certificates and agree to repay the original amount plus a small amount of interest at the end of a fixed term, referred to as a maturity date. Even though these certificates pay interest, they are considered a form of saving, and not a form of investing. Purchasing a CD is not taking on any significant risk because you are not directly investing in any company and the certificates are insured by the Federal Deposit Insurance Corporation (FDIC) for up to $250,000.

Interest rates vary based on market conditions, term length, and amount deposited. Most certificates require a minimum deposit of $1,000 but can be as large as $250,000 and term lengths vary from three months to five years. Usually, longer terms and larger certificates will result in higher interest rates. Often these interest rates can be less than the real rate of inflation, so keeping large sums of money wrapped up in CDs means you may slowly lose purchasing power.

The biggest disadvantage with using a CD as a method of saving is the penalty for early withdrawal. This prevents you from using a CD to store emergency funds and should only be used for holding large sums of money that are to be used at a specific future date, such as saving for the down payment on a home, college tuition, purchase of a vehicle or to cover the cost of a wedding.

Money Market Accounts

A money market account is a type of savings account with a bank or credit union that pays higher interest than a regular savings accounts and allows you to write a limited number of checks and easily transfer money like a checking account. Most banks require a minimum deposit of $10,000 or more and you must maintain a minimum balance to avoid monthly fees, which can be as high as $50 per month. The higher interest rates and large minimum deposit make it similar to a CD, but unlike a CD, there is no maturity date or penalty for withdrawals, making your funds far more liquid and easily available to cover large expenses quickly.

The interest rate is variable based on the current market. Typically, accounts requiring larger deposits and minimum balances offer the highest and most competitive interest rates. Money market accounts are best suited for storing money to cover large, unpredictable expenses and is a good place for your 3-6 months of emergency expenses. You can make large payments directly from your money market account or transfer money to a regular savings or checking account as needed to cover smaller day-to-day expenses.

ASSETS VS. LIABILITIES

"Rich people acquire assets. The poor and middle class acquire liabilities they think are assets."
—Robert Kiyosaki

While simple in definition, knowing the difference between these two key terms will be the difference between growing a substantial amount of reoccurring wealth that will last your family for generations or wasting your hard-earned money on consumer products that steal your wealth, making the American Dream feel more like a nightmare. The biggest problem is that most middle-class people confuse the definitions and often justify large purchases by considering the items assets, when they are really liabilities that drain them financially.

Assets

Assets are items you own that increase in (or at minimum maintain) value over time. Some assets will also produce income or pay dividends, such as investing in a company. Some examples of assets include:

- Stocks
- Bonds
- Land
- Commodities
- Rental properties
- Businesses

Liabilities

Liabilities are items that decrease in value over time and steal wealth from you, often in the form of fees, taxes, memberships, utilities, and maintenance costs. The assets listed above are straightforward, but let's dig into some common example of liabilities that many middle-class families think are assets.

- Your Home – Despite what most people believe, your primary residence is not an asset. Unless you are renting out a spare bedroom, it does not produce a regular income and will cost you thousands of dollars every year in property taxes and maintenance. While it's true that many homes go up in value over time, the increase is usually not enough to completely offset the true cost of home ownership. With that said, we all need a roof over our head and owning a home in the long run is almost always cheaper than renting. It's just important to recognize that your home is costing you money, not making you money.

- Vacation Properties – Vacation homes are typically considered liabilities as they are usually located far from your primary residence, which in turn causes you to hire out the maintenance. Vacation homes must be furnished, often lavishly, and are only rented out when not in use by the owners. They are typically also located in wealthy areas with high property taxes and in neighborhoods that often require HOA fees.

  Rental properties that are considered assets are typically located close to your primary residence, which allows you to do your own maintenance and check up on the property from time to time. They are not furnished, are repaired with low cost materials, and are available for rental year-round producing a regular source of income.

- Cars, Motorcycles, Boats, and Planes – Just about anything with a motor will depreciate over time. These mechanical devices, while fun to own, and in some cases a necessity for our daily commute, are a slow drain on our finances.

- TVs, Computers, and Game Systems – A $5,000 flat screen may feel like an "investment" when buying it, but don't be fooled: in just a few years it will be for sale in the neighborhood garage sale for a few hundred dollars or less. Technology loses value faster than almost anything else we purchase.

Retire Early, Retire Rich

INVESTING

"Someone's sitting in the shade today because someone planted a tree a long time ago."
—Warren Buffet

To be wealthy you need to invest your money and make it work for you. Start by breaking your habit of thinking like a consumer and begin thinking like an investor. Consumers make purchases with no regard for their future value. Investors analyze every purchase and choose items that will best hold, or increase, in value over time.

This becomes even more important when dealing with large sums of unexpected wealth, such as an inheritance or a work bonus. The consumer might celebrate newly acquired wealth by taking a vacation, going out for an expensive dinner at a fancy steak house or buying a new car. Not only do they waste the money, but they typically spend more than the value received.

- As an example, let's say someone with a consumer mindset receives a $5,000 performance bonus at the end of the year and they decide to buy the hot tub they've always wanted. They select a model that's $5,000, but after taxes, fees, accessories, delivery, and installation, it ends up costing $6,000. So not only did they waste the entire bonus on an item that will depreciate in value, but they spent more than the bonus and might have to put the $1,000 difference on a high interest credit card. In addition to the upfront cost, it will also cost nearly $50 a month to heat and maintain for the life of the hot tub. With a life span of up to 20 years, the true cost of the hot tub when you factor in the opportunity cost will be over $52,000! This is an example of an item which most people think is an asset but is actually a liability that robs them of their wealth.

Someone with an investor mindset would instead use the money to pay down the principal on their mortgage, make a necessary home repair, invest in the stock market, or start a 529 college savings plan for their children.

- As an example, let's say that same $5,000 performance bonus is given to someone with an investor mindset and they instead use the money to pay down a portion of the principal on their home mortgage. Assuming a 5% interest rate, that $5,000 payment will reduce the interest payment by $250 every year over the entire duration of the loan, saving them up to $5,000 over that same 20-year period and helping them pay off their home years sooner.

Just this simple example of two people with different views on how to handle money produced a difference in net worth of $57,000 from just one work bonus! Imagine if they acted similarly for every bonus, every paycheck, and every dollar they spend over the course of several decades. It becomes much easier to understand why some middle-class families can retire early with millions in net worth while others work their entire lives with nothing to show for it.

Compound Interest

Albert Einstein described the power of compounding interest as the 8th wonder of the world. If you understand its power and how to make it work in your favor, you are setting yourself up for a life of great reward. Thanks to compound interest, the value of $1 might be $5-10 at retirement. By getting into debt, not saving, and not investing, you are robbing your future self. Spending $30,000 on a new car in your 20s could buy a $300,000 condo at retirement. An expensive trip to Vegas could pay for an entire year of tuition for a child or grandchild. The key to taking full advantage of compound interest is to start investing as early as possible. Let's look at a fictional story comparing the financial journey of Money Savvy Mark and Debt Slave Dave.

At the beginning of the journey, Mark, like most young adults, has little career experience but is able to find a modest paying job. Mark is savvy with money, understands compound interest, and has time on his side. By working overtime and living below his means. He is able to invest $1,000 per month into his retirement account. He does this for just 10 years, contributing a total of $120,000 and never invests another penny. Using a historical stock market average growth of approximately 7%, his $120,000 investment will grow to a remarkable $1.4 million by age 60.

Dave takes a different path towards retirement, spending the first 20 years of his career living paycheck-to-paycheck, spending beyond his means, and making no attempt to save for the future. At age 40, he has the typical midlife crisis, realizes he's way behind preparing for retirement and decides to catch up. For the next 20 years, he maxes out his 401(k) by contributing $18,000 per year for a total of $360,000. By age 60, he only has $800,000 in his retirement account.

The power of compound interest allows Mark to accumulate nearly double the nest egg as Dave, even though he only contributed one-third as much towards his investments (see *Figure 1 – Compound Interest*). Mark has also put himself in a position where, if desired, he can retire years earlier than Dave while still having a much larger nest egg.

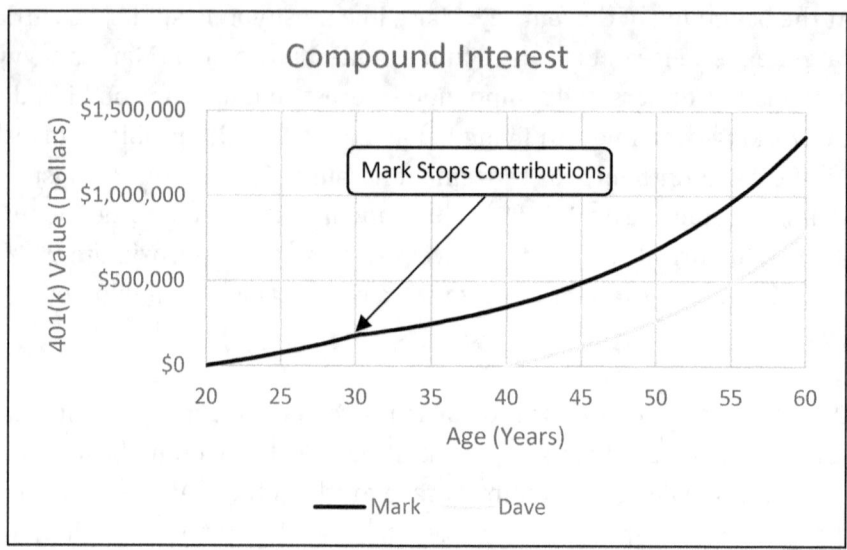

Figure 1 – Compound Interest

Stocks

The term "stock" is derived from the method of using a piece of wood, called a "tally stick" to record financial records in England and parts of Europe during the late medieval period. Flat sticks were split in half and the interest and term length were recorded on both sides. The issuer, usually a bank, kept one half called a stock and the lender kept the other half called a "foil", the receipt needed to collect their interest. The unofficial areas where banks and wealthy investors gathered to trade their wooden tally sticks eventually became known as stock markets.

Today, stock represents partial ownership (albeit generally a very small piece) of a company, their assets, and the profit they produce. There are two main ways to profit from stock ownership.

- Dividends – Companies split profits with shareholders.

- Speculation – This method does not focus on profitability of a company, but rather the stock price which is expected to go up in value and allow the shareholder to sell for a profit.

Investing in individual stocks is best kept to a small portion of an investment portfolio since it is risky to keep all of your wealth in one single asset. When buying stocks, don't try to time the market. That is a losing strategy since no one has a crystal ball, and it is impossible to know exactly when there will be fluctuations in the market. Remember, even the stock brokers on Wall Street, who make multi-million-dollar salaries, have insider info, and political connections, don't know when the market will go up or down.

Pensions

A pension is a retirement benefit plan funded by the employer on behalf of the employee. Most pension plans meet the IRS requirement for tax deferred investment and allow them to grow tax free until withdrawals are made. This type of retirement plan is typically guaranteed by the employer to pay out a certain pre-determined amount at retirement to the employee, regardless of the value available in the investment account or current performance of the market. At one point, nearly half of all private sector employees in the U.S. were covered by pension plans. Today, the private sector has transitioned to the use of 401(k) plans, allowing employers to transfer the responsibility of financial contributions and the long-term risk of growth (or lack of) on to the employee.

Unlike a privately held retirement account, with a pension you must work a certain number of years to become "fully-vested" before you qualify to receive full benefits at retirement; this is typically 25 years or greater. You also have no control over how your funds are invested and usually can't collect your pension until a set age without significant penalties, typically 60 or greater. As a result, pensions are usually not conducive of early retirement or financial independence.

401(k)

A 401(k) is a tax advantage retirement savings plan offered by most private sector employers that allows employees to automatically deduct and invest a portion of each pay check. A 401(k), like a mutual fund and many other group stock market investments, is managed by a financial advisor. Fees charged can vary widely based on the financial institution offering the fund, along with the type of fund selected, but typically they charge around 0.5% to 1% per year. Be sure to take advantage of any 401(k) match program your employer offers; it's getting paid to save. As of 2017, over half of all 401(k) plans offer an employer match, with 50% up to 6% being the most common, meaning your employer will contribute 50 cents for every dollar you contribute up to 6% of your income. Using a numeric example, if you make $100,000 a year and contribute 6% of your income for a total of $6,000, your employer will contribute 50 cents per dollar up to 6% so they will contribute an additional $3,000 (see *Figure 2 - 401(k) Contributions*).

Pre-Tax Income	401(k) Contribution	Employee Contribution	Employer Match	Total 401(k) Contribution
$100,000	2.0%	$2,000	$1,000	$3,000
$100,000	6.0%	$6,000	$3,000	$9,000
$100,000	10.0%	$10,000	$3,000	$13,000
$100,000	18.5%	$18,500	$3,000	$21,500

Figure 2 - 401(k) Contributions

Individuals with incomes less than $120,000 are limited to $18,500 in contributions per year (check IRS.gov for the latest contribution limits) while Individuals making greater than $120,000 per year are classified as "High Earners" capping their deduction at 5% of their income and $18,500 total per year. It's important to note that employer contributions are not limited to $18,500, allowing employees that max out their 401(k) to be able to contribute greater than $18,500 per year.

There are two different 401(k) plan options:

- A traditional 401(k) is funded with pre-tax dollars which allows for tax free growth and is only taxed when you make withdrawals from the plan during retirement. The advantage to the traditional 401(k) is that most people are in a higher tax bracket during their working years, but when they retired they earn little or no income putting them in a lower tax bracket, allowing them to keep more of the money they invested.

- A Roth 401(k) is similar to a traditional 401(k), but is funded with post-tax dollars, grows tax free, and the withdrawals are not taxed during retirement. The 2018 contribution limit of $18,500 applies to both traditional and Roth 401(k) accounts, however, since the taxes on a Roth 401(K) are paid up front it will give you more purchasing power at retirement. Another advantage of a Roth 401(k) is that is does not require you to take mandatory withdrawals at age 70½ like a traditional 401(k). This allows you to keep more tax-free money in the market for longer.

The main disadvantage of using a 401(k) for retirement investing is the inability to withdraw your money from the account until you reach 59½ years of age. While it is possible to withdrawal money from your 401(k) prior to 59½, there will likely be a 10% penalty plus additional taxes unless you meet very specific financial or health requirement. How to avoid early withdrawal penalties and structure your investments for early retirement are covered in *Chapter 11: Early Retirement.*

It is possible to contribute to other retirement accounts in addition to your 401(k), such as an Individual Retirement Account (IRA). The question is whether those contributions will be tax-deferred money. Unfortunately, many high-income earners may not qualify for a tax deduction. Often, people who are able to max out their 401(k)s are likely to exceed those income thresholds.

If you've reached the maximum amount of 401(k) contributions, you have what most people consider to be a "first world problem". If you are fortunate enough to have this problem and still have excess money, you can invest the remainder in mutual funds, index funds, or other taxable accounts as they have no dollar limits. However, these accounts should only be funded AFTER you've maxed out your 401(k) and IRA accounts as taxable accounts are purchased with after-tax dollars and the gains will be taxed when sold.

IRA

An Individual Retirement Account (IRA) is a tax advantage account fund intended for retirement saving. An IRA is a privately funded account that is held and managed by a bank or other financial institution, whereas a 401(k) is offered directly through an employer. Individual taxpayers are allowed to contribute 100% of any earned income up to the limit of $5,500 (as of 2018). Contributions to a IRA may be tax-deductible depending on your income, tax-filing status and other factors. Be sure to reference the latest IRS tax codes or contact a financial advisor for the latest contribution limits and restrictions.

There are two different IRA plan options:

- A traditional IRA is funded with pre-tax dollars, allows for tax free growth, and is only taxed when you make withdrawals from the plan during retirement. The advantage to the traditional IRA is that most people are in a higher tax bracket during their working years, but when they retired they earn little or no income putting them in a lower tax bracket, allowing them to keep more of the money they invested.

- A Roth IRA is similar to a traditional IRA, but is funded with post-tax dollars, grows tax-free, and withdrawals are not taxed during retirement. Since the taxes on a Roth 401(K) are paid up front it will give you more purchasing power at retirement.

The most notable disadvantage of using a IRA is the contribution limit, approximately 1/3 that of similar 401(k) plans, along with the inability to withdrawal funds from the account prior to 59½ years of age. However, the Roth IRA does include two important differences:

I. It requires that the first contribution to be made at minimum of five years before the first withdrawal. Meeting this requirement allows you to fund your account with post-tax dollars and make tax and penalty free withdrawals during retirement.

II. It allows plan holder to withdrawal just the contributions portion of their investment, penalty and tax free before 59½ years of age. This withdrawal exception will be key to several early retirement strategies that will be explored in detail later in this book.

If you are an employee of the Federal government, you will likely have access to a Thrift Saving Plan (TSP). This investment functions similar to private sector retirement plans, allowing employees to easily move non-government related IRAs and 401(k) plans into a TSP and vice versa upon employment changes.

Thrift Savings Plan

A Thrift Savings Plan (TSP) is a defined contribution plan that provides United States Federal civil service employees, retirees, and members of the military with retirement savings benefits. A TSP is designed to closely resemble the 401(k) plans available to private sector employees, allowing employees to develop a personalized retirement plan based on their age and retirement goals. The plan allows for matching contributions by government agencies, automatic contributions via payroll deductions, and are popular because of their low fees. Employees also have the ability to move non-government related IRAs and 401(k) plans into or out of their TSP upon employment changes.

Unfortunately, like a 401(k) the plan requires you to be 59½ years of age before making penalty free withdrawals.

A TSP is very important for government employees who are looking to achieve financial independence without being reliant on a pension or other pre-determined source of retirement income not under their control. A TSP allows government employees to choose their savings rate, how their funds are invested, and take steps necessary for a penalty free early withdrawal.

There are currently 10 funds available for selection:

- G Fund - Government Securities fund.
- F Fund - Fixed Income Index fund.
- C Fund - Common Stock Index fund.
- S Fund - Small Capitalization Stock Index fund.
- I Fund - International Stock Index fund.
- L2050 - Retirement date of 2045 and thereafter
- L2040 - Retirement date between 2035 and 2044
- L2030 - Retirement date between 2025 and 2034
- L2020 - Retirement date between 2015 and 2024
- L Income - Individuals currently receiving monthly payments

For additional information regarding TSP fund options visit: www.tsp.gov/InvestmentFunds/FundOptions/index.html

Mutual Funds

A mutual fund is a popular investment tool that allows a large group of investors to pool their money to purchase a diverse portfolio of stocks, bonds, commodities, and other wealth producing assets. By investing in a mutual fund, you are also gaining the skills and knowledge of a professional financial advisors who can purchase assets at discount rates, constantly watch the market, and properly manage a large diverse portfolio of assets to a level that the average person could never possibly achieve.

The main disadvantage of a mutual fund is the fees associated with managing the fund. High fees can eat away at the returns on your investment and over the course of decades can add up to tens of thousands of dollars in lost value. However, just because a fund has high fees doesn't necessarily mean it's a bad choice. In some cases, higher fees may equate to a better managed fund that regularly produces higher returns on your investment, just make sure you compare the fees being charged with the historical rate of return on that investment to make sure you are getting what you pay for. Additionally, by purchasing mutual funds, you are giving up some control of how your money is being invested. For most this is a relief, allowing you to know your hard-earned money is in good hands.

For those seeking early retirement, you can invest in mutual funds directly through your bank or various financial institutions such a Vanguard. Unlike a 401(k), where you invest through your employer, a mutual fund has no restrictions on contribution limits or age of withdrawal. Dividends earned from a mutual fund you have owned for less than a year are taxed at your income tax rate, but dividends paid by mutual funds held for a year or longer are taxed at the Long-Term Capital Gains Rate which is significantly less. (See *Figure 3 – 2018 Income and Capital Gains Taxes*)

Income Tax Bracket	Long Term Capital Gains Tax Rate
10%	0%
12%	0%
22%	15%
24%	15%
32%	15%
35%	15%
37%	20%

Figure 3 – 2018 Income and Capital Gains Taxes

Fees

Almost all actively managed investment funds will charge small yearly fee for their services, typically listed as the "expense ratio" on your financial statement. Most investors become overly focused on asset allocation and overlook hidden costs and how they will impact the long-term performance of their investment. The fees vary but are typically around 1% or less per year for most actively managed mutual funds. You may also have a personal financial advisor managing your money who may charge up to 1% as well for a potential totally of 2% of yearly fees. Your yearly fee is calculated based on the <u>total value of the portfolio, not just your earnings</u>. Financial institutions make money off your portfolio whether it goes up or down in value. At first glance, this seems like a small, almost insignificant amount, but like all forms of interest, the effects are compounded exponentially over time.

As an example, let's take a typical year with a historic average stock market return of 10%. To find your real growth you must first subtract the historical average inflation rate of approximately 3%, then subtract the fund and management fees, varying from 0-2% total, leaving you with 5-7% real growth (see *Figure 4 – Net Earnings*).

Gross Earnings	Inflation	Total Fees	Net Earnings Less Fees & Inflation	Percentage of Net Earnings
10.0%	3.0%	0.0%	7.0%	0.0%
10.0%	3.0%	0.5%	6.5%	7.1%
10.0%	3.0%	1.0%	6.0%	14.3%
10.0%	3.0%	2.0%	5.0%	28.6%

Figure 4 – Net Earnings

How much difference will fees really make? Over a long period of time even a small fee of 1% or less can massively erode your earnings, potentially giving away hundreds of thousands of dollars in profits. Let's use the above percentages and apply it to a $100,000 one-time investment over a 30-year period (see *Figure 5 – Investment Fee Comparison*).

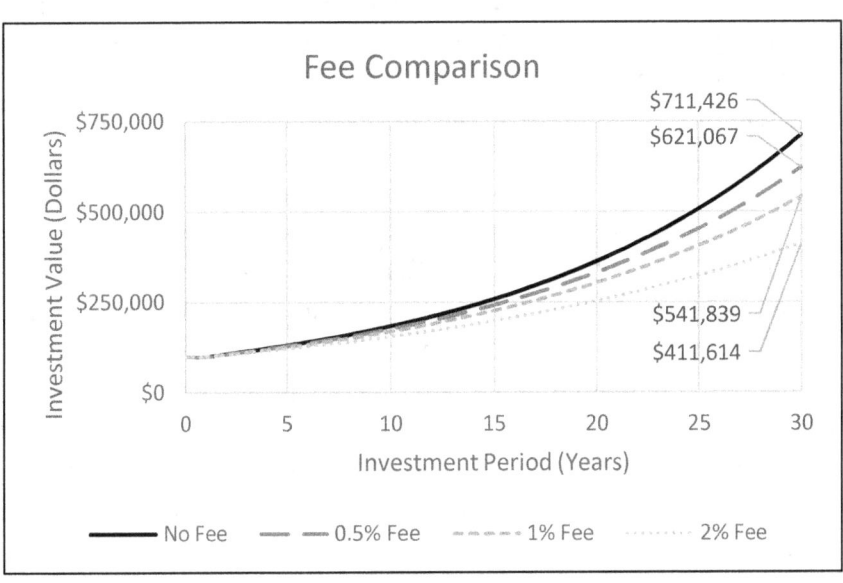

Figure 5 – Investment Fee Comparison

At the end of the 30-year period a 0.5% fee will cost you $90,359 in inflation adjusted dollars. As the fees increase up to 1% or even as high as 2% you could be giving up as much as $359,812, that's over half of the value of your investment without fees!

So why do investment companies charge fees for actively managed investment accounts? These fees cover the operating cost of the company and the wages of the employees who are working hard behind the scenes actively researching thousands of publicly traded companies, compiling data on their earnings, long term track records, and earnings forecast to determine which stocks to buy and sell. While you are at work, home with your kids or taking the dog for a walk there are bankers and investment advisors working to increase the value of the mutual funds and other investments they represent, in theory producing earnings beyond what the market can produce. However, most financial advisors rarely beat the market long term.

While fees must be minimized to maximize earnings, investors should always stay focused on their personal needs first when selecting an investment. If you are close to retirement, don't select a high-risk investment just because it has lower fees. The need for a less volatile investment on the short-term outweighs all lost earnings due to high fees.

Investors seeking the lowest fees possible should consider choosing an index fund, a type of mutual fund that is designed to track the whole market, rather than target specific sub-markets or attempt to achieve a desired level of growth or risk. The main advantage of index funds is the low fees compared to actively managed funds. The average fee for an index funds is 0.09%, with some as low as 0.04%, compared to 0.82% for the average mutual fund. Financial institutions can offer these lows fees on index funds because of minimal trading and management requirements compared to actively managed mutual funds.

Tax Loss Harvesting

Tax loss harvesting is the process of selling one investment with the intention of recording a capital loss that can be used as a deduction on your taxes. The key is that an investor takes the money from the sale and re-invests it into a nearly identical asset with similar performance. Note that the IRS will not allow investors to write off tax losses if a "substantially identical" investment is purchased within 30-days of the sale. While there is no way to get around this with an individual stock, it is commonly used with mutual funds and other stock market derived investment funds as there are countless funds to choose from and the distribution of assets within funds vary widely, with many offering similar performance.

If your capital losses realized are more than your capital gains for a certain year, you can deduct the difference as a loss on your tax return. The current IRS limit for capital loss deduction for 2018 is $1,500 for individuals or $3,000 for married couples filing jointly. Any losses realized beyond the limit can be carried over and deducted from future tax returns indefinitely until the total value of the loss has been deducted. Let's look at an example:

- Say have $100,000 invested in Mutual Fund A, and it drops in value to $90,000. You would sell Mutual Fund A, realizing a $10,000 capital loss. You immediately buy $90,000 worth of Mutual Fund B, a fund that is similar to Mutual fund A. When you go to file your tax return for that calendar year you can deduct $3,000 of the $10,000 as a capital loss, the remaining $7,000 can be deducted on future tax returns.

    Savvy investors may have already noticed that by buying Mutual Fund B at a lower price they you will eventually be paying taxes on a larger capital gains. This is true, so why does it make sense to go through the hassle?

As part of this example let's say several years go by and both mutual funds A & B grow in value from $90,000 to $120,000. If you stuck with Mutual Fund A you would pay 15% taxes on a $20,000 profit. If you instead harvested your tax loss and reinvested in Mutual Fund B, you will pay the same 15% capital gains tax on the larger $30,000 profit but will be able to reduce your income tax by $10,000 which is typically taxed at a rate much higher than 15%.

Keep in mind the IRS does not require you to report gains or losses until an investment is sold, known as a "realized" gain or loss. This gives you complete control over your investments, allowing you to decide when is the optimal time to sell for maximum profits or losses. A patient investor with a large portfolio can sell their investments at the lowest possible value during a recession or financial crisis, immediately reinvest, and realize losses worth tens of thousands that can be used in the future to offset income tax at 25% (or higher) in exchange for paying the 15% capital gains tax on a larger capital gain. Investors in the highest tax brackets will see the greatest financial benefit from using tax loss harvesting. This is just one of many ways the rich are able to reduce their tax burden.

Bonds

Bonds are a debt-based security issued by private corporations or government entities that pay a fixed amount of interest per year. The face value is the original amount borrowed and is paid back in full to the borrower upon the maturity of bond, plus an annual or semi-annual fixed interest rate, called a "coupon rate". The interest payments are referred to as "coupons" because generations ago bonds were originally issued as physical pieces of paper and the bond holder would have to remove a portion of the bond, the coupon and turn it in to receive the interest payment. While bonds pay a fixed interest rate, the value of a bond on the open market will fluctuate based on current interest rates of new bonds being issued.

For instance, a $1,000 bond with a 5% interest rate will sell for less than $1,000 on the open market if new bonds are being issued with interest rates greater than 5%. If new bonds are being issued with interest rates less than 5%, the existing bonds will trade for greater than $1,000 as investors are willing to pay a premium for an investment with a higher interest rate. The popularity of bonds also tends to be the inverse of stocks, as money flows to the higher returns of the stock market during good financial times and when the returns on stocks becomes negative, such as during a recession, investors move their money to bonds where they are guaranteed a fixed positive interested rate. Bonds are typically good for short term stability, but they lack the large long-term growth of the stock market or other investments. Bonds are best used when you are approaching the later years of your career or during retirement, when you can afford to give up some reward in exchange for less risk in your investments.

Alternative Investments

For most people, traditional investments such as a 401(k), mutual funds, stocks, and bonds will be their primary form of investing to growth wealth and will account for much of their net worth at retirement. As you grow large sums of wealth it can be a good strategy to diversify your investment portfolio by acquiring alternative investments.

Alternative investments are assets held outside of the typical investment tools of stocks and bonds. You will not collect dividends or profits from a company's earnings like you would with a traditional investment. You are instead speculating the value will increase in the future, allowing you to sell them for a profit. Alternative investments include, but are not limited to; venture capital, private equity, hedge funds, real estate investment trusts, and commodities as well as real tangible assets such as precious metals, numismatic coins, collectible cars, fine wine, art, and firearms.

In some cases, alternative investments can also be part of a hobby. When using a hobby as an alternative investment, keep in mind there is potential for volatility in the popularity of many hobbies so it's a good rule of thumb to limit these assets to less than 10% of your net worth. A good example of a once popular hobby and alternative investment that has dwindled is stamp collecting. The internet has all but eliminated the need to mail letters and purchase postage. As a result, younger generations are not picking up collecting stamps as a hobby and people with high dollar stamp collections have experienced a massive depreciation in value.

Inflation

When developing your long-term investment strategy, it's important to not overlook the negative forces that impact your ability to grow wealth. Inflation is the slow and steady devaluation of our currency, decreasing its purchasing power, and causing prices of everyday items to increase.

Fortunately, the US dollar has experienced very minimal inflation over the last 100 years compared to many nations, with the historical average being around 3% per year. Inflation rates have at times peaked as high as 15% but were primarily due to excessive government spending during World Wars I and II and the poor Federal economic policies of the 1970s.

When calculating the future value of an investment its best to use the "real interest rate" which is simply the return on investment minus the rate of inflation. For example, if you take the historic average stock market return of 10% and subtract the historic average inflation of 3%, you get a 7% real interest rate. 7% is a conservative percentage to use when calculating long term stock market investment growth.

Precious Metals

The ancient Egyptians began using gold as a medium of exchange as early as 5,000 BC. Since then almost every major civilization has utilized gold and other precious metals as a form of currency, allowing for easier trade and creating a somewhat standardized monetary system among various cultures from all parts of the world. The ancient Greeks were the first to create gold coins of uniform size and weight, making monetary transactions even more efficient, critical for an empire spanning multiple continents.

Precious metals remained the primary currency for thousands of years until the modern global gold standard was ended in 1971. This was the result of nations turning in their holdings of over-printed and inflated US dollars in exchange for the undervalued gold bullion being held at the Federal Reserve. Then president Richard Nixon was forced to end the gold standard, decoupling the US dollar from the nation's gold reserves to prevent depletion. Despite the lack of a gold standard, the US government and many other nations around the world still maintain stockpiles of precious metals as tradition, a hedge against hyperinflation, and political bargaining power.

Since the end of the gold standard, precious metals have been available for purchase on the open market and are considered by some to be a good long-term investment and a hedge against hyperinflation. Whenever a recession or high inflation looms, investors return to gold as a safe haven, often pushing prices to new record highs, only to see the price collapse a few years later when the economy recovers.

Since the gold standard ended in 1971, the price of gold has risen from $44.60 an ounce to well over $1,000 per ounce, providing an average yearly return of approximately 7.5%. But unlike stocks and other forms of investment, gold is a commodity and does not produce anything of value, nor does it pay dividends. Instead, it is used to protect against hyperinflation and maintain value during uncertain economic times. Like other commodities, such as a barrel of oil or a bushel of wheat, future gold prices are based solely on what others are willing to pay for it and what the perceived future value will be. Because of gold's inability to produce wealth beyond itself and a historically volatile market, it is recommended not to put a large portion of your investment portfolio into precious metals holdings, typically no more than 10%.

529 College Savings Plan

This tax-advantage financial plan is operated by state or educational institutions and allows for easier saving and access to college education and post-secondary training. A 529 plan can have one or multiple designated beneficiaries which can be a child, grandchild, friend, relative, or even yourself. While there is no specific limit as to how much you can contribute to a 529 plan per year, if the plan is setup for someone other than yourself or a dependent, any contributions over $14,000 per year will be subject to the IRS gift tax. While it is called a savings plan, it really falls into the investment category as contributions to the 529 plan can invested in mutual funds, bonds, and money market accounts.

A 529 plan is funded with post-tax dollars and earnings and withdrawals are not subject to Federal or state taxes as long as the funds are used for qualified education expense such as tuition, books, fees, or room and board. When applying for financial aid, a 529 college savings plan in you or your child's name must be reported on the Free Application for Federal Student Aid (FAFSA) as investment assets and can reduce the amount of financial aid received. Typically, assets located in a pension, 401(k) or other retirement accounts are not reported on the FAFSA and will not count against you. The potential loss of financial aid should not be used as an excuse to not save for your child's education. If you follow the principals outline in this book you will likely grow enough wealth that you will not qualify for financial aid, making the effects of a 529 plan on the FAFSA irrelevant, instead you will have the necessary assets to cover the cost of tuition.

What if your child (or other beneficiary) decides not to attend college?

- The funds are not locked in the plan and can be withdrawn, but any deductions from the plan for non-qualifying education expenses will be subject to income taxes plus an additional 10% penalty.
- You can add a beneficiary to the plan and use it to pay for their educational expenses to avoid the fees and taxes.
- The plan is not limited to college expenses; it can be used for any type of post-secondary education and vocational schools.
- There is no requirement for when deductions must occur. If a child decides not to attend college, you can leave the funds in the plan and add a grandchild as a beneficiary later.

Education

Investing in yourself is one of the best strategies for becoming wealthy and successful. There are endless studies indicating a college graduate will earn more than someone with just a high school diploma, yet there are plenty of millionaires with little or no formal education. While post-secondary education is a necessity for those seeking a professional career, it's important to remember that education doesn't always come in the form of a piece of paper and learning doesn't have to occur in a classroom. Some of the more important life skills you learn will be from real world experience.

Reading is a fabulous and inexpensive way to learn new skills, increase your productivity, and bring value to your life. The key to financial success is increasing your knowledge and skill base. Spending just 30 minutes a day reading will vastly increase the amount you learn and can be a great way to relax at the end of a day. Reading this book is an investment in your future, providing you with the financial skills necessary to get out of debt, save and invest large sums of money, and create passive income, all allowing you to retire early and retire rich. Make it a goal to read several non-fictions books a year – some useful genres include:

- Automotive repair
- Biographies
- Carpentry
- Cooking
- Ethics
- Exercise
- Finance
- Gardening
- History
- Home improvement
- How-to
- Investing
- Leadership
- Relationships
- Science
- Self-help
- Technology

Taking skill-based classes is another great way to better your life. Whether it's a fitness class at your local community center or a cooking class at a community college, there is always something new you can learn no matter your age.

The internet, in particular YouTube, is an excellent source of free educational information. In a matter of minutes, you can learn how to change the oil in your car, replace an electric socket, build a deck, unclog a drain or solve any number of everyday problems you face. Tasks that used to require consultation or an appointment with a high paid technician can be handled by yourself with just a little time and research. The more you know, the less you must pay others to do tasks for you. Just be sure to seek out multiple reputable source, as information on the internet is often only worth what you pay for it.

HOME OWNERSHIP

"It's easy to underestimate the real cost of home ownership."
—Suze Orman

For most American middle-class families buying a home will be the largest single purchase they make in their entire lives, yet most have little to no knowledge of the process or what it takes to make home ownership a good financial decision.

Buying a home, be it a first, second, or more, is an exciting event. But it's easy to get overwhelmed by the process, which can result in making a poor decision that you will be forced to live with for years. Be sure to slow down and take your time, only go as fast as you are comfortable with and be sure to ask lots of questions along the way. Remember, there are nearly a million new homes built in the Unites States each year and aside from a few select large urban hot spots there is no shortage of homes available for purchase. Don't be in a rush. If you miss out on that home you liked it's ok, there are dozens, maybe even hundreds just like it where you live that are currently listed or will be up for sale soon.

When hunting for a good deal, you must learn to remove emotions from the home buying process. Part of a realtor's sales tactic will be to make you develop an emotional connection with the home they are selling, even trying to convince you that other potential buyers are interested in the home and that you must act fast (preferably paying full price) if you want to secure the home of your dreams. Making a quick, impulse decision to buy a home based on how it makes you feel can be financially disastrous.

One of the first financial mistakes people make when looking to purchase a home is buying more than they can afforded. <u>Buy what you can afford, NOT what the bank is willing to lend you.</u> The bank's primary goal is to make a profit from the interest you pay on the money they loan you. They have little concern for what you can afford to pay. Buying a home beyond your budget can mean years of working overtime, arguments over money, picking up a second job, delay investing in a 401(k), making it difficult to save for your children's education, and can even lead to foreclosure or bankruptcy.

Sustaining an expensive mortgage is fine when times are good. A strong economy often means lots of overtime, pay raises, and performance bonuses, making it easy to afford that massive multi-bedroom with the large backyard overlooking the lake in that expensive neighborhood (with an extra high property tax rate) where you always dreamed of living. But life is cyclic and easy times are often followed by hard times. People change careers, get laid off, family members get sick, or must take an unpaid Family Medical Leave of Absence. Many of these situations seem extreme and are easy to pass off by saying...

"That will never happen to me!"

But bad things will happen, and they tend to occur at the worst times possible. Even a wonderful blessing like the birth of a child can create tension in a marriage if the mortgage consumes such a large portion of their income that it prevents a parent from being able to take off time to raise a child.

The easiest way to avoid over spending is by come up with a price range BEFORE you start looking for homes and make sure to stick to the budget. Start looking at homes at the bottom of your price range. Use that as a baseline and if you are not satisfied with what is available, you can always go up in value and still be in your price range. Most home buyers almost always end up spending more than what they originally budgeted for, so starting your home search at the top of your price range almost guarantees spending more than you can afford. Instead start looking at homes at the bottom of your price range and work your way up until you feel you are getting a home that meets all your needs.

Accounting for the home purchase and all the ongoing costs is important since there will be many fees and expenses not accounted for in the listed price, such as closing costs, moving expenses, property taxes, home owner's insurance, and monthly Home Owners Association (HOA) fees. Some of these expenses are reoccurring and potentially add hundreds of thousands of dollars to the purchase price of a home over several decades of ownership. Take for example an average HOA fee of $500 per month. It will cost you $6,000 a year and $60,000 for every decade you live there. If you instead would have taken that same $500 a month and invested it in the stock market over a 30-year period, it would be worth over $600,000!

Renting vs. Owning

Deciding whether to rent or own a home is a major decision that can have a large impact on your short and long term financial situations. Unfortunately, there is no universal right or wrong answer when it comes to buying vs. renting, as both can make financial sense depending on your situation. The cost of a home mortgage will typically be less, on a month to month basis, than renting an equivalent sized home in the same location. But, there can be large upfront costs associated with home ownership, including the down payment and reoccurring costs that may include property taxes, utilities, repairs, insurance, and other expenses that a renter would not normally be expected to cover.

Renting is typically favored among younger adults, as they lack the savings, credit history, and high-income necessary to secure a home loan. Statistically, people in this age bracket are not yet married, do not have kids, frequently change careers, are active, adventurous, and are not ready to settle down in one location. You pay a premium to rent, but this allows you flexibility to follow your job, friends, family or other interests. If your employer reassigns you to an office several states away or you suddenly have the urge to move to New York City, you can do so on a moment's notice without the baggage of having to sell your home. Most rental agreements will typically include a clause that allows tenants to get out of a lease if their employer is requiring them to relocate or they changed jobs and the new position they take is a certain distance away from where they are currently renting or working. The only money you will need up front to rent is a security deposit, usually equal to one month's rent. A rental will be move in ready and some even come fully furnished; perfect for someone traveling to a new country or being relocated for a short period of time. There is no need to paint rooms, replace carpet, repair the broken screen door or fix that leaky roof that was missed during the home inspection. Additionally, the lack of home maintenance allows you to travel without worrying who will mow the lawn, rake the leaves, or shovel the snow.

A home is massive commitment, but it can also be extremely financially and emotionally rewarding. Buying a home is best suited for people who have put down roots and are comfortable with staying in one place for a long period of time (see the following section regarding the Five-Year Rule). Anyone who owns a home knows that no matter the season there are always repairs to be made and yardwork to be completed. When a pipe breaks or a drain is clogged, it's the owner's responsibility to fix it, which usually involves a trip, or two, to the hardware store. Spending an entire Saturday fixing a broken dishwasher would have been a miserable task when I was in my 20s, but now I look forward to the task and the rewarding feeling of fixing something. Maybe it's because replacing a $5 latch can save me a $150 bill from a technician, or maybe it's the pride of maintaining my own home. Either way there is an emotional connection to a home you own that often isn't present when you rent. It's the place we come home to every night, its where we feel safe, where our children grow up, and the equity that grows over the years will help build the foundation for our retirement. But it's important to minimize the amount of interest paid on your home mortgage. A large down payment and an aggressive payment schedule will make it possible to quickly build equity and not have it negated by the cost of interest that accumulates over a long loan period.

30-Year vs. 15-Year Mortgage

The easiest way to reduce the total amount of interest paid on a home is to go with a 15-year mortgage rather than the more common 30-year; this will make your monthly payments significantly higher but will pay off your mortgage in half the time and save you tens of thousands of dollars in interest.

The amount of interest you pay on the money the bank loans you is an exponential calculation. Such that even a small increase in the loan interest rate and/or duration can massively change the total amount of interest you pay.

- Fortunately, in today's financial market we are seeing record low interest rates on home loans, typically 3-5%. Which is incredible, considering only a few decades ago mortgage interest rates were double digits.

- The same compound interest that can be used to make your money work for you and passively grow your wealth can, however, work against you in the form of debt. Even a seemingly low 5% interest loan, over a 30-year period, will effectively double the cost of your loan. With banks accepting lower and lower down payments recently, it pays to remember that every dollar borrowed now will accumulate debt in the years ahead.

Figures 6 – 11 provide a comparison of 15-year and 30-year mortgage loans using 3%, 4%, and 5% interest rates.

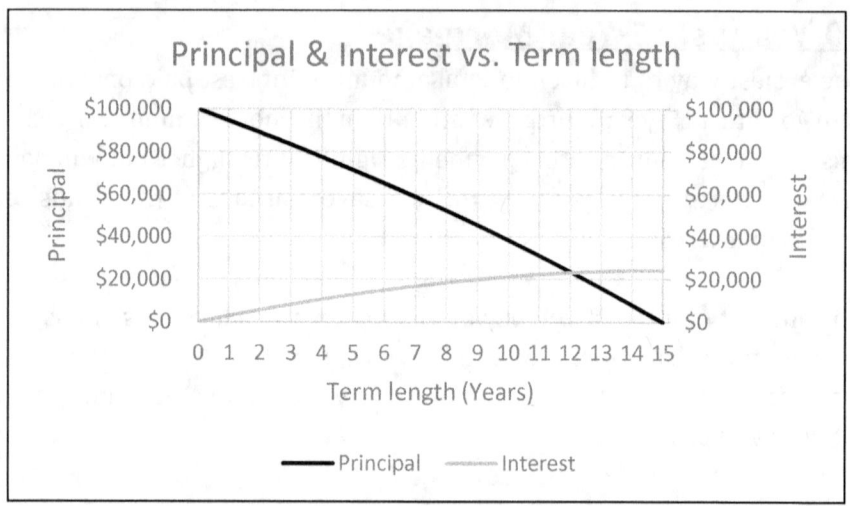

Figure 6 – 15-Year Loan with 3% APR

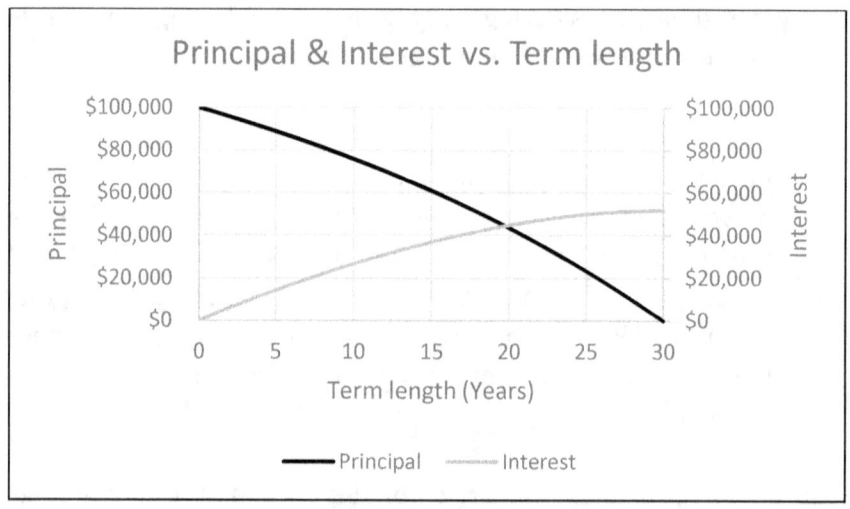

Figure 7 – 30-Year Loan with 3% APR

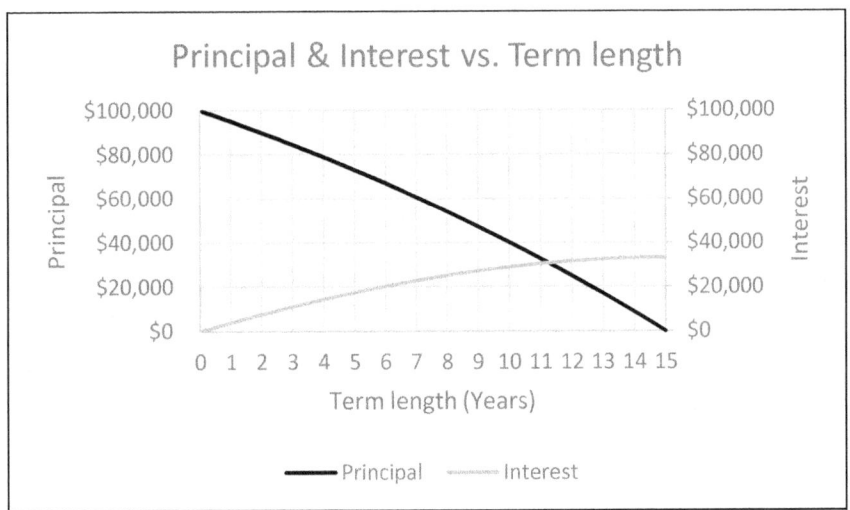

Figure 8 – 15-Year Loan with 4% APR

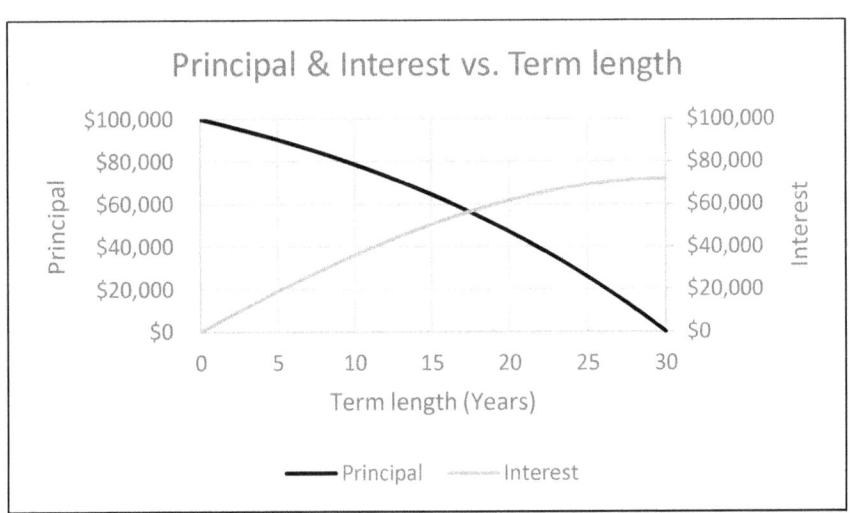

Figure 9 – 30-Year Loan with 4% APR

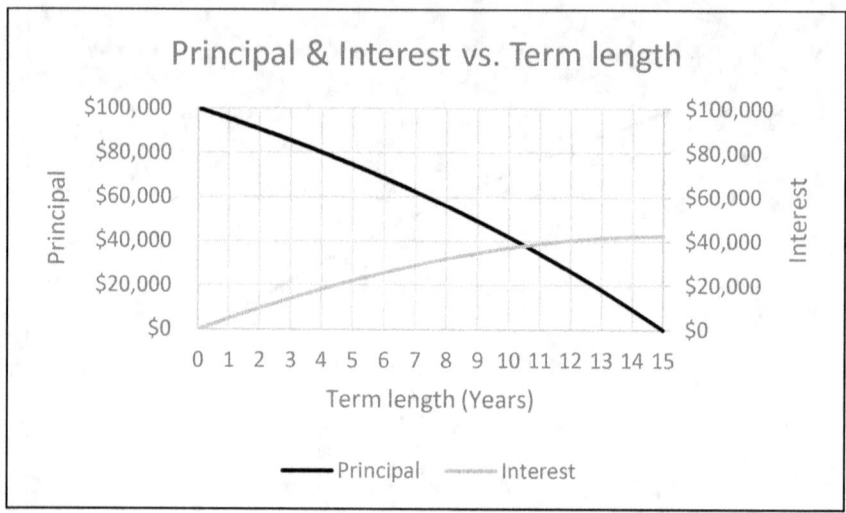

Figure 10 – 15-Year Loan with 5% APR

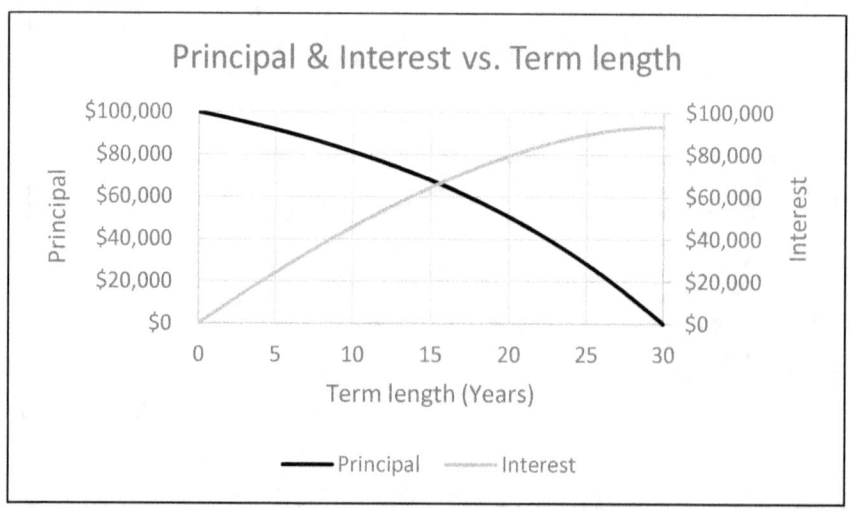

Figure 11 – 30-Year Loan with 5% APR

Loan Refinancing

Stop! Don't do it!

Most home mortgages are structured to be a fixed payment month to month throughout the duration of the loan, allowing home owners to more accurately budget their expenses, which increases the chance the bank will receive payments in full and on time. What the banks don't tell you is that not every payment is created equal. The very first mortgage payment is composed primarily of interest that is paid to the bank, with only a fraction of the payment going towards paying off the loan principal. As the years go by and you pay down the principal of the loan less of each payment goes towards paying interest, until your final payment which is entirely principal. See *Figure 12 – Mortgage Payment Breakdown vs. Year*, for an example of a 30-year, $100,000 mortgage at 3% interest.

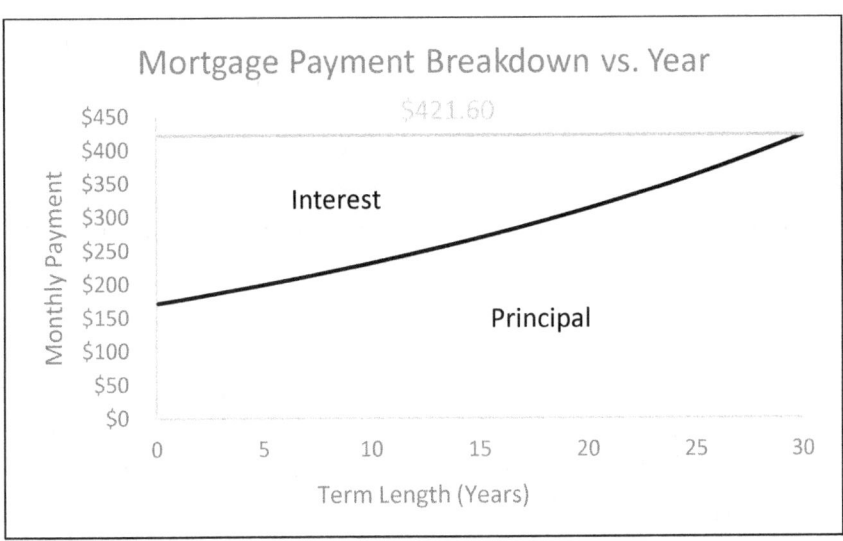

Figure 12 – Mortgage Payment Breakdown vs. Year

Retire Early, Retire Rich

To better understand why it often doesn't make sense to refinance, lets imagine a board game called "Mortgage" It has 30 spaces and the rules state each player is allowed to move forward one space per turn. During the game you can draw cards, one of which is the "refinance your mortgage" card and it states:

REFINANCE YOUR MORTGAGE

Move back to the start of the board and move two spaces per turn.

Drawing this card earlier in the game will be a benefit but if drawn late in the game will be a hinderance, causing you to start over despite being only a few spaces from the finish.

Refinancing a loan is simply the process of taking out a new loan to pay off an old loan. No matter where you are in the process of paying your original mortgage, refinancing will start you back at the beginning of the payment cycle with a brand new 30- or 15-year loan. You will be back to paying large amounts of interest each month, and even though the monthly payments are less, the total amount of interest paid over the duration of the loan will be more.

Mortgage brokers may also encourage you to take out extra money to make upgrades to your home such as remodeling your kitchen, replacing an old deck or installing an inground swimming pool. If you hesitate they will remind you:

"It's only adds $50 a month."

What they don't say is its $50 a month, every month, for the next 30 years! They may also inform you that refinancing is a great way to "pay off" your debt. Don't be confused, nothing is being paid off, taking out a low interest long term loan to pay off a short-term loan with only a slightly higher interest rate is not a cure for debt.

So, when does it make sense to refinance?

- If you bought the home within the last few years and you can refinance at a rate 1-2% lower than your current interest rate it may make sense. In this situation the lower interest rate, while small, if applied over several decades will amount to a significant reduction in interest paid.

- If you can refinance with a lower interest rate and shorter term, you'll be able to save money. Say for example you are 10 years into a 30-year 5% mortgage. Refinancing with a 15-year 3% mortgage would be a wise decision, allowing you to pay off your home five years sooner and save thousands in interest.

Let's look at four different scenarios of a hypothetical home buyer who borrowed $100,000 for the purchase of a home, to help better analyze when it makes sense to refinance a mortgage.

- Scenario 1 is a typical 30-year loan period at a 5% interest rate. This scenario assumes the borrower pays the loan off in full over a 30-year period without refinancing and will be used as the control for comparison. At the end of the 30-year period the borrow pays a total of $93,256 in interest on a $100,000 loan (see *Figure 13 – Scenario 1 – No Refinance*).

- Scenario 2 assumes the borrow refinances their original 30-year 5% loan after 5-years with a new 30-year loan at a slightly lower interest rate of 4%. At the end of the 35-year period the borrow pays a total of $90,005 in interested on a $100,000 loan, for a total savings of $3,251 (see *Figure 14– Scenario 2 – Refinance at Year 5*).

- Scenario 3 assumes the borrow refinances their original 30-year 5% loan after 25-years with a new 30-year loan at a slightly lower interest rate of 4%. At the end of the 55-year period the borrow pays a total of $109,937 in interested on a $100,000 loan, for a total loss of $16,681 (see *Figure 15 – Scenario 3 – Refinance at Year 25*).

- Scenario 4 assumes the borrow refinances their original 30-year 5% loan after 25-years with a new 15-year loan at a lower interest rate of 3%. At the end of the 40-year period the borrow pays a total of $96,407 in interested on a $100,000 loan, for a total loss of $3,151 (See *Figure 16 – Scenario 4 – Refinance at Year 25*).

Loan	Duration (Year)	Interest Paid	Interest rate	Starting Balance	Ending Balance	Monthly Payment
1	30	$93,256	5%	$100,000	$0	$537

Figure 13 – Scenario 1 – No Refinance

Loan	Duration (Year)	Interest Paid	Interest rate	Starting Balance	Ending Balance	Monthly Payment
1	5	$24,038	5%	$100,000	$91,829	$537
2	30	$65,967	4%	$91,829	$0	$438
Total	35	$90,005				

Figure 14 – Scenario 2 – Refinance at Year 5

Loan	Duration (Year)	Interest Paid	Interest rate	Starting Balance	Ending Balance	Monthly Payment
1	25	$89,493	5%	$100,000	$28,447	$537
2	30	$20,444	4%	$28,447	$0	$136
Total	55	$109,937				

Figure 15 – Scenario 3 – Refinance at Year 25

Loan	Duration (Year)	Interest Paid	Interest rate	Starting Balance	Ending Balance	Monthly Payment
1	25	$89,493	5%	$100,000	$28,447	$537
2	15	$6,914	3%	$28,447	$0	$196
Total	40	$96,407				

Figure 16 – Scenario 4 – Refinance at Year 25

Scenarios 3 and 4 clearly highlight how refinancing in the later years of a mortgage rarely makes sense. Unfortunately, most borrowers see the lower interest rate and monthly payment and assume refinancing will save them money.

Even in Scenario 2, where the total interest paid is reduced (compared to the Scenario 1), you must include the cost of refinancing the loan (3-6% of the loan principal) along with expenses such as property appraisal and a title search. These fees can add up to thousands of dollars, completely canceling out any money you might think you are saving.

The bottom line is refinancing a home mortgage can make sense in certain situations, but the average home owner is often just paying off one loan with another, delaying becoming debt free, and putting more money in the bank's pocket.

Five-Year Rule

Home ownership can be both emotionally and financially rewarding if done correctly. When buying a home, you should always consider how long you are planning to remain in the home. If you enjoy exploring new cities every few years, are active duty military, or are temporarily relocating for work, taking on the financial commitment of home ownership may not be the best financial decision. One way to help decide if buying a home is the right choice is to consider the five-year rule. This rule is the approximate number of years a home buyer must own a home before the value of the property appreciates enough to offset the numerous costs associated with buying and selling the home, allowing the seller to break even on their purchase price. While not set in stone, it is typically more common for the seller to cover the 3-6% realtor commission. Additional costs may include advertising the property, surveying property lines, deed research, home inspection, moving furniture, and temporary lodging and storage.

While historic trends show homes increasing 1-2% per years annually, this growth rate is not guaranteed. Many housing markets are very volatile and can see frequent boom and bust cycles over short periods of time. Buying at the top of the market with little or no down payment can put you in a situation where you owe more on the mortgage than the current market value of the home. It will take several years of mortgage payments for a home owner to lower the principal of their loan enough to allow them to sell their home at the now lower market value. Even if the value goes up, there are still many expenses that make owning a home for less than five years undesirable.

Home Buying Tips

- A rough guideline is that your monthly mortgage should be no more than one-fourth of your after-tax household income. Ideally you should be able to afford your mortgage, and all of your basic living expenses on a single income. Be sure to use extra caution if one income is seasonal work, sales/performance based, or has other large fluctuations in pay.

- Always pay for a professional home inspection. No matter what the home owner or real estate agent may say, paying a couple hundred dollars for a professional inspection can potentially save you tens of thousands of dollars in repairs by discovering issues with the home before it's too late.

- Some common items an inspector should look for are:

I. Plumbing — Leaking/clogged sinks, adequate water pressure, and the condition of the exterior sewer lateral or septic tank, including damage from tree roots.

II. Moisture — The presence of moisture can cause the growth of black mold. Moisture is most commonly found in basements due to cracked walls and in attics.

III. Electrical Wiring — The wire material should be copper, not aluminum, sockets should be grounded in bathrooms and kitchens, and utilize a modern circuit breaker box.

IV. Heating and Cooling — Check the furnace installation date and life span, amount of insulation, and test for carbon monoxide leaks.

V. Exterior — Determine the condition of the roof shingles, and remaining life span. Look for rotting wood, broken bricks, missing mortar, holes, gaps or other damage to the homes siding. Review condition of the driveway, deck and other exterior structures such as awnings.

VI. Security Features — A home security system is a plus but at a minimum they should assess the condition of the doors, windows, locks, exterior lighting, and confirm the presence of quality smoke and carbon monoxide detectors.

- While title insurance is rarely needed, it will protect you against any unforeseen issues with the title or ownership rights of the property once purchased. It is inexpensive and if it is needed it could save you tens or even hundreds of thousands of dollars. Title insurance, like any kind of insurance is used to cover the value of high dollar items you can't afford to lose, repair, or replace.

So, what could possibly wrong with the title?

I. The previous owner may have been elderly and forgot to pay property taxes for the last few years or the owner lost their job and were avoiding paying them for financial reason. These back taxes must be paid before ownership of the property can be transferred.

II. During a divorce, there may be be an agreement allowing one of the spouses to continue living in the home on the condition that if the home is sold the profits will be equally divided. In some rare cases the spouse will sell the home without informing their ex-spouse, with the intent of keeping the money for themselves. This has the potential to create a lawsuit once the ex-spouse realizes the home has been sold.

III. There may be a lien on the property that the owner forgot about, failed to disclose or was not discovered at the time of sale. A lien is a notice placed on the title of the property saying the current owner owes someone money, usually to a creditor for unpaid debt, but it could also be for services rendered that were not paid for. This may include an expensive repair to a home such as replacing the furnace, cutting down a large tree, repairing weather damage or the installation of a driveway, deck, or inground pool. Going to court to get a lien placed on the property title will prevent it from being sold until the lien is removed, meaning the owner will have to pay up if they ever plan to sell their home.

IV. Undisclosed or unrecorded easements can be a headache for home owners. What would you do if you discovered there was a utility easement on your property and the local energy company wanted to run a gas line through your back yard, or a large shed? Or your detached garage had been built by one of the previous owners without acquiring a permit and is located over the top of a large sewer line that the city must replace. The owner of the utility easement is not legally responsible for replacing any fences, buildings, or landscaping located in the easement meaning you will be responsible for paying out of pocket to replace it.

- Whether you're looking to buy or sell, having a home appraised is highly recommended and may be required by some lending agencies. As a seller you know you won't be leaving money on the table nor will you end up with a home that is stuck on the market for an extended period of time. As a buyer an appraisal is a quality assurance check verifying your offer is fair based on the condition of the home and the current market.

- Private Mortgage Insurance (PMI) is an insurance policy that covers a lender in the event of a mortgage default. Originally introduced to the financial market in the 1880's, it has been used throughout the last 100 years, but it has gained great popularity recently after the 2008 financial crises as banks now utilize the insurance, paid for by the buyers, to protect them from the risk of default by sub-prime (high-risk) buyers.

    While many have hailed PMI for its ability to allows buyers with minimal savings to get into the home of their dreams, it is not recommended by most financial advisors. PMI must be purchased whenever a home buyer has less than a 20% down payment and will add approximately $50 a month for every $100,000 of loan value. It is a general guideline that if a buyer can't afford the 20% down payment they are likely not in a position to afford the home or the hidden expenses associated with home ownership.

- A mortgage contingency clause allows a buyer to back out of a deal if the bank does not agree to extend a loan or if deficiencies are discovered, such as structural damage, that may be identified during the appraisal process. Work with your realtor to develop a list of concerns to be outlined in the contingency clause.

- If you're looking to get the best deal possible, consider buying during the winter to take advantage of the seasonal variations and avoid the jump in housing prices often seen during the summer months. As the weather heats up so do home prices. Warmer weather creates more activity at open houses, and parents with grade school children are looking to quickly close a deal to get their family settled in before the new school year, and are willing to pay a premium to do. While there are good deals to be found, keep in mind shopping for a home during the winter is kind of like shopping the clearance rack at the department store, you will have limited selection and there may be a reason why no one else was willing to close on the home.

- Being able to look passed undesirable cosmetic features that are easily fixed can save you money. While ugly paint, crazy wall paper, and shag carpet may be a deal breaker for most people, it can be a great way to find a bargain on a well-constructed home that will end up being a solid financial investment. For a few thousand dollars you can carpet and paint an entire home. I have seen home owners with a little motivation and a vision turn a home with an undesirable tiny back yard and no privacy into a dream backyard retreat just by adding a privacy fence and a little land scaping.

- Having the biggest, nicest or most expensive home in the neighborhood may be a source of pride, but financially it is often a bad decision. Homes that typically see the most appreciation in value are those priced at or below the average home price in the neighborhood. There is usually high demand for lower priced homes in good neighborhoods as there is a larger pool of buyers available who willing to pay a premium to live in a trendy area, safe neighborhood or have access to a good school district.

Home Maintenance

Homeownership can be very rewarding but also a large time and financial commitment. The national average home maintenance cost is 2% of the home's value per year. For example, if you are considering buying a $100,000 home you can expect to pay approximately $2,000 per year on household repairs, maintenance and upgrades. It's important to remember that while some years you will have minimal or even no home maintenance costs, other years you will have significantly more than the average.

Keeping up with maintenance is not a budget item to skimp on. Small repairs will maintain the value of your home and will help you avoid larger costly repair in the future. Issues like cracked basement walls, leaking gutters, cracked driveways, or damaged window seals are cheap and easy to repair but if left unaddressed for a long period of time can result in damage to your home, requiring the use of professional repair services, and costing many thousands of dollars.

Home Insurance

Most home buyers put effort into making sure they get the lowest interest rate possible on their loan, but one common expense home buyers overlook is home insurance. Here are some tips that can save you hundreds of dollars a year:

- **Shop Around** – Get multiple quotes to assure you are getting the best rate as they can vary significantly from company to company. If there is an insurance agency you would prefer to work with, but they don't have the lowest rate, give them a copy of your lowest quoted price from a competing insurance company and ask if they are willing beat or at least match it. I would recommend shopping around for quotes every few years to make sure you still have the best deal possible.

- **Deductible** – Remember, the purpose of insurance is to cover the cost of large expenses you can't afford. As your net worth and emergency fund increases over time you should consider increasing your deductible to help lower your premiums.

- **Bundle** – We've all heard the cheesy ads about bundling our home and auto policies, but it's a legitimate cost savings method. Insurance agencies are willing to reduce premiums in exchange for additional data on their consumers, plus those who bundle are more likely to stick with their insurer and will be their first choice for future insured items such as motorcycles, RVs, and vacation homes (when you're financially independent, of course!).

- **Discounts** – Be sure to mention the following items as they are common discounts offered that your agent may forget to ask you about:

    I. Senior citizen
    II. Non-smoker
    III. Proximity to fire hydrants/services
    IV. Home security system
    V. New roof
    VI. New electrical wiring
    VII. Good credit score
    VIII. Storm shutters (in hurricane prone areas)

Cost Saving Tips

- Learn to be a handy man. Performing your own household repairs and maintenance can save you tons of money. Simple household repairs like unclogging a stuck drain, cleaning gutters, replacing light bulbs, painting walls, staining decks, sealing cracks in a drive way, etc... are all easy tasks. Most local hardware store should have any tools or materials you need, and a quick web search will provide everything you need to know before tackling small projects.

- Use Angies's list, HomeAdvisor or similar contractor referral websites to find reputable contractors at the best price. Service providers are rated by their customers, giving you a transparent view of their quality of work and how they threat their customers.

- Barter services with friends, family, and neighbors. Offer to help a friend move in exchange for them helping you cut down a dead tree.

- Share tools with <u>trusted</u> friends or family. Tools can be very expensive and often not used more than once or twice a year. You might be able to borrow your neighbor's rototiller to plant your garden in the spring, in exchange for letting them borrow your leaf blower in the fall.

Retire Early, Retire Rich

EARLY RETIREMENT

> *"The question isn't at what age I want to retire, it's at what income."*
> —*George Foreman*

According to U.S. Census Bureau data, the average retirement age for full-time workers in the U.S. is 63 years old.

With no minimum age for retirement why do people wait until so late in life to retire?

The short and simple answer is they have not achieved financial independence. Those who are unable to cover their basic living expenses in retirement must work until they qualify for government assistance programs to care for them such as, Social Security at age 62 and Medicare at age 65. This is not unique to the United States, both developed and undeveloped nations all over the world have similar high age requirements for receiving government assistance during retirement.

If you desire to retire early you must take a different financial path in life, one of saving, investing, and most importantly self-reliance. There are also growing concerns over the government's ability to keep Social Security and Medicare funded as more people are retiring from the work force than are entering it, increasing life expectancy, and medical costs that continue to rise at a rapid rate.

Retirement Gap

The retirement gap is the period between when you retire from your full-time position and when you are able to collect healthcare and financial benefits tax and penalty free.

If you are planning to retire early with a pension you will need to bridge the gap between your desired early retirement age and when you can start collecting your pensions penalty free. The ideal way to do this is to plan ahead and invest a small portion of your income into mutual funds or other privately held investments which have no age requirement to access them, allowing you to retire from your position once you are fully vested and be able to cover living expenses until your pension becomes available. The larger the retirement gap, the more you will need to have invested outside of your pension. If you are unable to save additional on the side or are already at your desired early retirement age you may need to consider working part-time in the private sector to cover living costs.

Similarly, if you are working in the private sector and are invested in a 401(k) you may want to consider putting a small portion of your retirement investments into mutual funds or other privately held investments towards the end of your career. These investments will be taxed at a higher rate than a 401(k) but can be accessed at any age, allowing you to bridge the retirement gap. If you do have a large portion of their retirement savings locked up in a 401(k), IRA or other tax advantage accounts there are a handful of methods you can use to make early withdrawals and not be penalized.

Traditional 401(k) & IRA Early Withdrawal

The most common way Americans save for retirement is via tax advantage retirement savings accounts. The details and restrictions of each plan vary but they all have a common goal of helping middle-class Americans prepare for retirement by allowing tax free growth of their investment assets. Unfortunately, our financial and retirement system was not designed with early retirement in mind and the average American grossly under estimates how much money they will need to support themselves during retirement. As a result, the IRS imposes fees and taxes on early withdrawals from retirement accounts with the hopes of discouraging people from cashing out their account unnecessarily early. Despite the government's best intentions, not everyone is looking to withdrawal from their 401(k) to fund the purchase of a mid-life crisis sports car. Some have diligently saved to become financially independent and just want to quit the rat race. The good news is there are a handful of ways you can tap into your tax advantage retirement accounts without triggering any penalties.

Qualified Distribution – One way to make penalty and in some cases tax free withdrawals from your tax advantage retirement savings account is to meet the IRS requirements for qualified distributions. The methods listed below will work with an IRA, but may not be possible with all 401(k) plans, and will vary based on the rules of your individual plan. However, your 401(k) can be rolled over into a IRA after retirement regardless of age. Common IRA and 401(k) qualified distributions are:

- Disability

- Death (not a recommended retirement strategy) allows for inherited retirement savings accounts to be withdrawal before age 59½ without being subject to the 10% penalty.

- Medical insurance coverage.

- Reimbursed for medical expenses. The funds must be used to cover medical expenses above 10% of your adjusted gross income. Easily achieved if you are retired without a source of income.

- Educational expenses for yourself, spouse, children or your grandchildren.

- First time home buyers can withdrawal up to $10,000 penalty free from their IRA penalty free. It doesn't technically even need to be your first home, you just can't have owned a home in the last two years. The money also doesn't have to be used for your home, as it can be used towards the purchase of a home for a child, parent or grandchild. While this method doesn't necessarily put spending money directly into your hands it's a way to reduces the cost of buying a home or help family members without paying with post-tax dollars from your bank account. Keep in mind this early withdrawal method may be penalty free but not necessarily tax free. There will be taxes applied to any distributions taken from a traditional IRA, just like you would have received after age 59½ because it was funded with pre-tax dollars, but if the distributions are taken from a Roth IRA, which is funded with post-tax dollars there will be no taxes at the time the distributions are taken.

- Military reservists can withdrawal money while on active duty without paying the 10% penalty.

Age 55 Rule – Many, but not all 401(k) plans allow employees who retired from their company after the age of 55 to take penalty-free withdrawals. Because contributions to the plan were made with pre-tax dollars any withdrawal will be considered taxable income, but it will not be subject to the 10% early withdrawal penalty. If you retire prior to age 55 you will have to wait until age 59½ to take penalty-free distributions. Any 401(k) plans from previous employers you left prior to age 55 will not be eligible for early withdrawal. If you are planning to use this rule to cover living expenses prior to reaching age 59½ do NOT roll over your 401(k) into an IRA, as this only works for select 401(k) plans.

Roth IRA Conversion Ladder – The Roth IRA Conversion ladder in its simplest form is a method that allows you to convert traditional 401(k) and traditional IRA plans to a Roth IRA, enabling you to take advantage of the IRS rules that permit penalty free early withdrawals from a Roth IRA under certain circumstances.

The downside is the IRS is aware of this loophole that allows for this type of conversion, which essentially defeats the purpose of the 10% early withdrawal penalty. So, the IRS imposes a five-year waiting period, which is sufficient to keep the average person from cashing out a portion of their retirement to pay for non-retirement expenses such as an expensive vacation or new car. While this may discourage most, all it requires is a little advanced planning for early retirees to use this method.

While it's possible to convert your entire IRA all at once, however, doing so would likely put you into one of the highest tax brackets. Its best to just convert one-year worth of future living expenses each year.

One easily noticeable problem is how to cover living expenses in years one through five while you're waiting to access the first amount of converted funds. There are a few ways to address this gap:

- Withdrawal funds from taxable accounts such as an index fund, mutual fund, stocks or bonds.

- Buildup sufficient funds in a high interest checking/savings account. Funds in these accounts may lose value due to inflation, but five years is a short enough period of time that inflation will have minimal impact.

- Previous Roth IRA contributions (not conversions) can be withdrawn at any time penalty free.

- If you already have funds in a traditional IRA you can convert them five years in advance of your anticipated retirement date.

- Get a part time job or side hustle for five years to cover your living expenses. If you are completely debt free you can actually live on a low paying part time job.

- Make withdrawals from tax advantage retirement accounts and pay the 10% penalty and taxes, while not ideal its only five years.

Let's breakdown the Roth IRA conversion ladder down into four steps:

1) After leaving your job for early retirement, you will be able to roll over your 401(k) into a traditional IRA. Most 401(k) plans should roll over directly into a traditional IRA, if not, you will have 60 days after cashing it out to deposit the funds into a qualified traditional IRA without penalty.

2) Convert one-year worth of living expenses from your traditional IRA to a Roth IRA. In doing so you will be required to pay taxes because you are making a withdrawal from a pre-tax retirement account. The same tax would apply even if you made a withdrawal after age 59½.

3) Wait five years. Each year convert an additional one-year worth of living expenses until you reach age 55, at which point you can stop conversions as you now have the funds in place to cover you through age 60, allowing you to make penalty free withdrawals.

4) After five years you can withdrawal the previously converted fund tax and penalty free.

The Roth IRA conversion ladder conversion is less complex than it sounds and is one of the most popular methods used in the early retirement community. For a better understanding of the yearly conversions that would take place for an early retiree, refer to *Figure 17 – Roth IRA Conversion Ladder* and *Figure 18 – Traditional 401(k) to Roth IRA Flow Diagram*.

Age	Traditional IRA to Roth IRA Conversion	Roth IRA Withdrawal
45	$50,000	$0
46	$50,000	$0
47	$50,000	$0
48	$50,000	$0
49	$50,000	$0
50	$50,000	$50,000
51	$50,000	$50,000
52	$50,000	$50,000
53	$50,000	$50,000
54	$50,000	$50,000
55	$0	$50,000
56	$0	$50,000
57	$0	$50,000
58	$0	$50,000
59	$0	$50,000

Figure 17 – Roth IRA Conversion Ladder

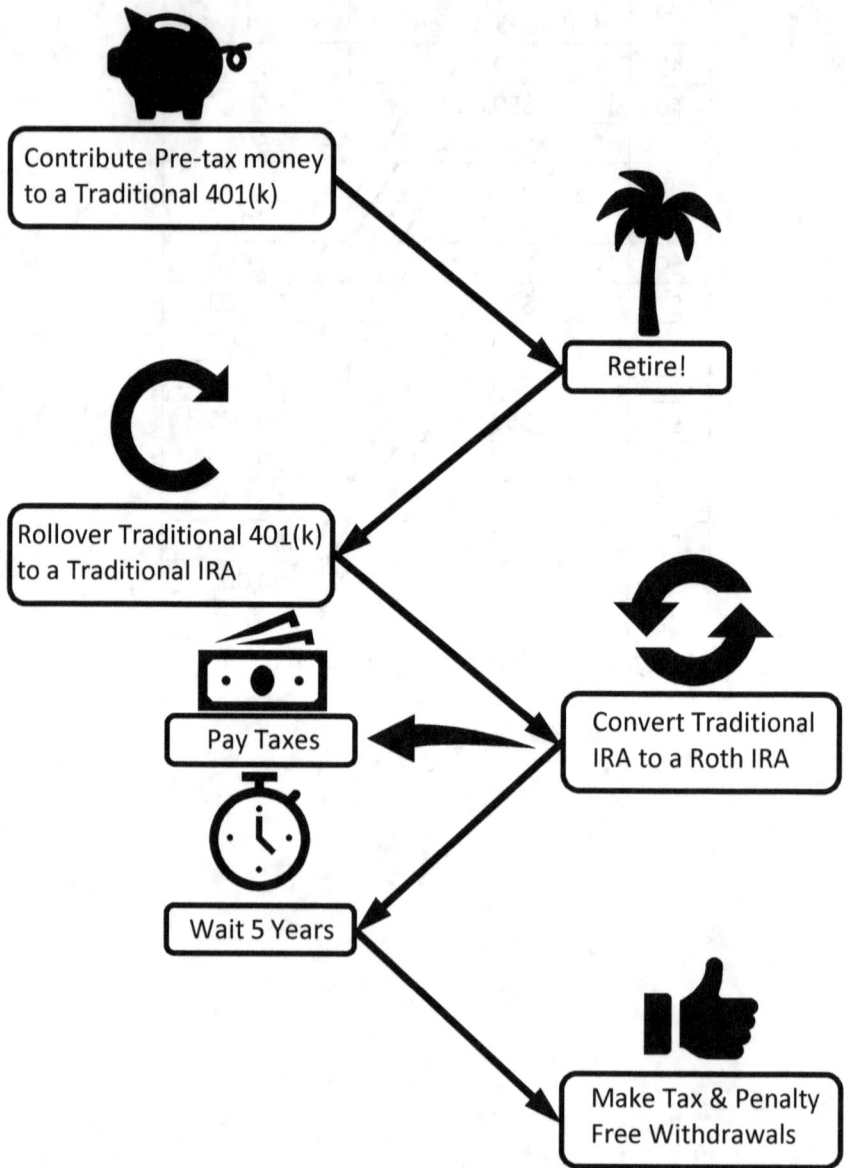

Figure 18 – Traditional 401(k) to Roth IRA Flow Diagram

72(t) Substantially Equal Periodic Payments (SEPP) – The IRS allows you to convert your retirement account into an annuity by agreeing to take substantially equal periodic payments based on your life expectancy, allowing access to your retirement savings without paying the 10% penalty. Once started you will be required to continue taking distributions for five years or until you reach age 59½, whichever is longer. If you are retiring less than five years prior to age 59½, you will be locked into taking the distributions until you hit the five-year minimum, even if the minimum time period extends beyond age 59½. If you retire significantly early, say in your 30s or 40s, you will be required to take distributions for multiple decades until you reach 59½ years of age. This could be a potential problem as it may be difficult to predict your yearly expenses decades in advance or adjust your withdrawal rate due to market fluctuations. Note that if you stop the withdrawals or withdrawal the incorrect amount you can be penalized for that year and all previous years, so it's very important to keep track of when you need to take distributions and for what amount.

The steps for using SEPP to withdrawal tax-advantages funds penalty free during early retirement are as follows:

1) When you leave your job for early retirement you will be able to roll over your 401(k) into a traditional IRA. Most 401(k) plans can be directly rolled over into a traditional IRA, if not, you will have 60 days after cashing it out to deposit the funds into a qualified traditional IRA without penalty.

2) Determine the amount of funds you will need per year during early retirement. Unlike the Roth IRA conversion ladder which allows you to select any amount, SEPP requires you to select from three different withdrawal rate options. Choose the withdrawal rate that fits closest with your predicted retirement spending.

3) Each yeah withdraw and pay taxes on that previously determined amount.

4) It is possible to adjust the withdrawal rate. However, the IRS limits you to making this change one time, so choose wisely.

5) Continue to make withdrawals for a minimum of five years or until you reach age 59½, whichever is longer.

There are three different methods for calculating your annual SEPP distribution:

- **Required Minimum Distribution (RMD)** – This method typically yields the smallest distribution of the three options but is the only method that varies annually and must be recalculated each year. The calculation is done by taking your current retirement account balance and divide it by your single life expectancy or joint life expectancy.

- **Fixed Amortization** – This method typically produces a distribution greater than the RMD method. The annual distribution is calculated by amortizing your account balance over your single life expectancy by using a uniform life expectancy table or joint life expectancy with your oldest named beneficiary.

- **Fixed Annuitization** – This method typically produces a distribution greater than the RMD method but is the most complex of the three methods. The amount of annual distribution is fixed and is calculated by taking your account balance divided by an annuity factor equal to the present value of an annuity of $1 per month beginning at the taxpayer's age attained in the first distribution year and continuing for the life of the taxpayer.

If you just went cross-eyed reading this last section don't worry, you aren't the only one. Using SEPP to access retirement funds can be complicated and as a result is not frequently used. Some of the methods for accessing early retirement funds penalty free often requiring you to plan many years in advance. For some this may seem overwhelming, rather than attempt to calculate these by hand, I recommend using one of the many free online calculators to compare the different methods to get a feel for which method would best fit your financial needs during retirement.

The best way to tackle your retirement plan is by breaking it down one piece at a time. Start by writing out your goals and develop a preliminary plan of action with an early retirement strategy you think best fits your needs. Then schedule an appointment with a financial advisor who has experience working with clients seeking early retirement and allow them to critique your plan and help guide you in the best direction based on your specific goals and life circumstances. I promise a few hours spent working with a financial advisor to develop an early retirement plan is better than working an extra 20 years, just because you felt the methods for penalty free early withdrawals were too complicated.

Roth 401(k) & Roth IRA Early Withdrawal

Since Roth retirement accounts are funded with post-tax dollars, an individual can withdraw up to the contributions amount from their account at any age without an early withdrawal penalty. Withdrawals of the earnings portion of the account cannot be made until the account holder reaches the age of 59½ and has had the account for a minimum of five years. Withdrawals of the earnings portion before age 59½ are subject to a 10% penalty and income taxes.

It is possible to make early withdrawals from a Roth 401(k) account; however, the rules and restrictions vary greatly based on the employer. Most employers will try to encourage employees to save for retirement by placing limits or outright preventing all pre-retirement withdrawals.

A Roth IRA is a privately funded, and early withdrawals rules are determined by the IRS, not your employer. As a result, a Roth IRA has significantly fewer restrictions and is an excellent source of early retirement funds, allowing the plan holder to withdrawal the <u>contributions</u> portion of their account, tax and penalty free, <u>at any age</u> if at least five years have passed since the Roth IRA account was established. Any withdrawals of the <u>earnings</u> portion of a Roth IRA prior to age 59½ will be subject to a 10% early withdrawal penalty.

Let's look at early retiree Earl as an example. Earl is 50 years old and has been contributing to his company Roth 401(k) for over a decade. At retirement his account is worth $350,000, of which $150,000 are his contributions and $200,000 are earnings. When Earl decides to retire early he is able to rollover his Roth 401(k) into a Roth IRA account after quitting his current job. Since he has had the "old" Roth 401(k) account for over a decade, it meets the five-year restriction, allowing him to begin making tax and penalty free withdrawals up to $150,000 (the <u>contribution</u> portion of his account) at any time. The remaining $200,000 (the <u>earnings</u> portion of the account) cannot be withdrawn until age 59½ without being subject to a 10% early withdrawal penalty.

For a better understanding of steps for accessing Roth retirement funds in early retirement, refer to *Figure 19 – Roth 401(k) to Roth IRA Flow Diagram*.

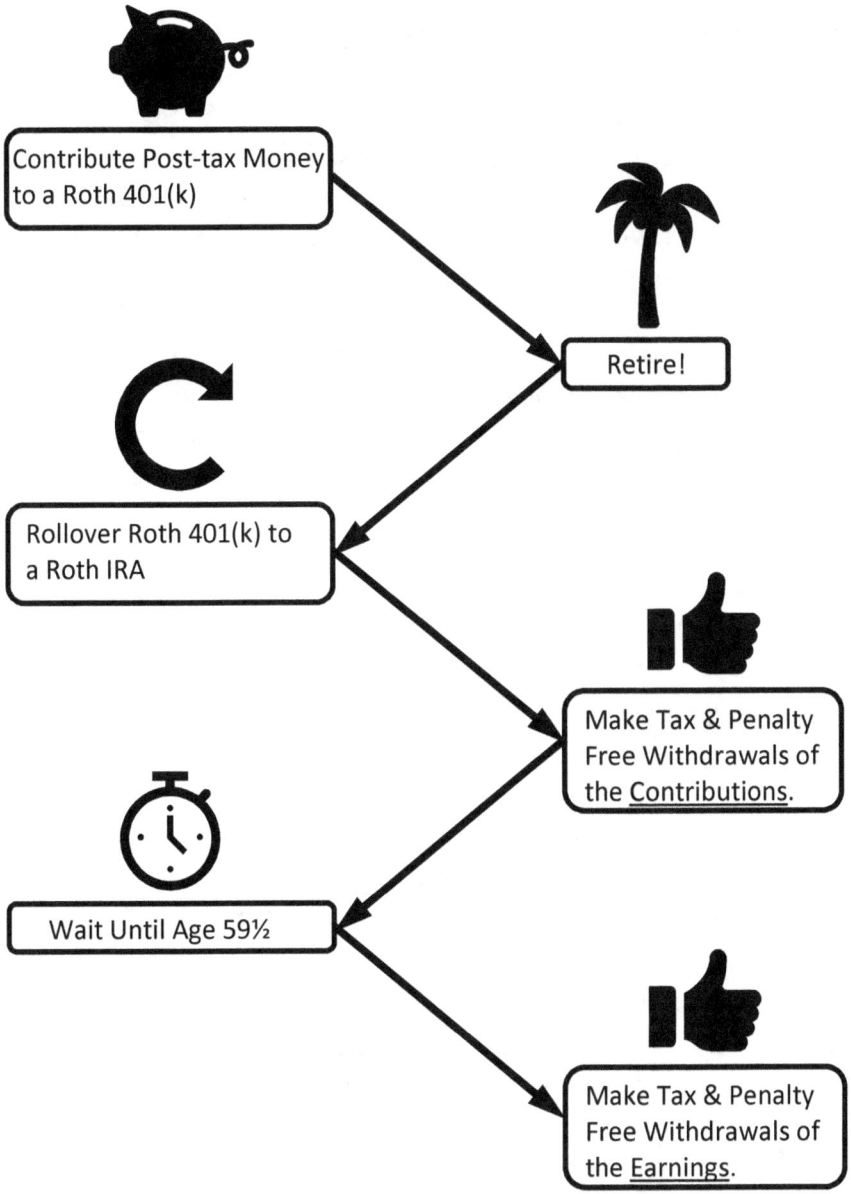

Figure 19 – Roth 401(k) to Roth IRA Flow Diagram

Investment Rate vs. Retirement Age

Your investment rate is the percent of your income contributed towards your retirement investments, such as a 401(k) or mutual fund. To increase your investment rate, you must subsequently decrease your spending rate and cost of living, by doing so you are also reducing the amount of money you will need to support yourself during retirement, allowing you to retire even sooner.

If you figured out a way to live on zero dollars a year you could retire right now, but if it takes 100% of your income to pay the bills than you will be unable to invest and will be forced to work indefinitely. This relationship can be seen in *Figure 20 - Investment Rate vs. Years Worked*.

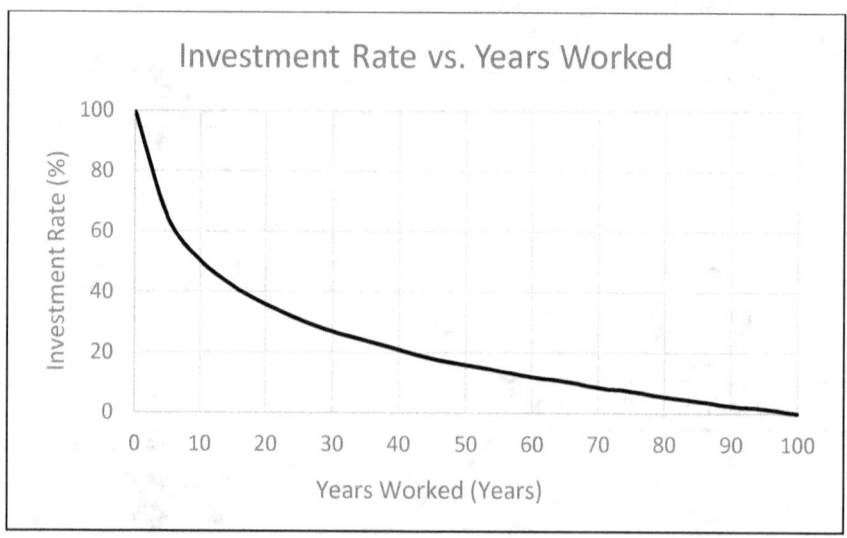

Figure 20 – Investment Rate vs. Years Worked

Four Percent Rule

One concern people have with early retirement is running out of money in their elderly years when they are unable to provide for themselves, especially a concern for those who have family members that typically live well into their 90s. This concern is addressed by using the four percent rule.

The four percent rule was developed by financial advisor William Bengen, who ran extensive calculations to determine the "safe" withdrawal rate based on historical growth rates of the stock and bond markets since the 1920's. It's intended to be a rough guideline when developing your investing strategy and determining how much principal you will need to have invested to minimize the risk of running out of money during retirement. By withdrawing a small amount of funds, equal to or less than the growth rate of your investment you should, in theory, never have to touch the principal of your investment and will have a steady source of income that will last indefinitely. Unlink a pension, which typically stop payments when the holder passes away, the principal of a privately held investment will remains available to be passed on to your heirs, and continue to grow if left invest.

When using the four percent rule, it's important to stick to it year after year, independent of what the market is doing, whether your investment has a positive or negative ROI you must still use a 4% withdrawal rate. If you exceed the withdrawal rate to cover a large expense, such as the purchase a vacation home, you run the risk of eroding the principal early in your retirement and decreasing the long-term performance of your retirement investment. You must also ignore the temptation to increase your withdrawal rates during years when your retirement investments are performing well above 4% as that growth is needed to offset years with negative performance in the future, allowing you to withdrawal the same 4% even when your investment accounts are going down in value during a recession.

Visualizing how much you need saved up for retirement can be overwhelming, especially for those who are young and just starting their careers or have spent a good portion of their lives in debt. But rather than look at a massive dollar amount that is likely decades away, keep it simple and break the goal down into smaller more achievable chucks.

A conservative estimate if you are seeking a traditional career path of 35 years and a retirement age of 60 or greater, would be to aim for 1x your annual income invested by age 30, and gradually work your way up to 25x your income by age 60 (see *Figure 21 – Conservative Investment Value by Age*).

Age (Years)	Investment (Income)
30	1x
35	2x
40	5x
45	10x
50	15x
55	20x
60	25x

Figure 21 – Conservative Investment Value by Age

A more aggressive approach if you are planning for early retirement, let's say age 45, would be to have 1x your annual income invested by age 25, and quickly work your way up to 25x your income by age 45 (see *Figure 22 – Aggressive Investment Value by Age*).

Age (Years)	Investment (Income)
25	1x
30	2x
35	4x
40	12x
45	25x

Figure 22 – Aggressive Investment Value by Age

Keep in mind the 4% rule is a rough guideline based on past performance, not a crystal ball into the future. Your retirement plan should be flexible and include a large emergency fund capable of handling six months or more worth of expenses to cover an unexpected job loss, medical emergency, or downward fluctuations of your investments. Your basic everyday expenses, such as food, utilities, rent/property tax, insurance, etc...should not exceed 2-3% with the remaining portion of the 4% covering discretionary spending such as, luxury items, dining out, and travel. This way if your portfolio takes a loss one year you can cut luxuries items, not basic living expenses.

The Actual Number

25x your current annual income invested is the rough rule of thumb used to determine how much you will need invested to use the four percent rule, but the exact amount will be different for every person.

If you are planning to live lavishly during retirement you may need significantly more than 25x, or you may need less if you are planning to live a more frugal lifestyle. Once you determine your desired annual retirement income you can use *Figure 23 – Retirement Income vs. Investment principal* to determine how much you will need invested to achieve that yearly income.

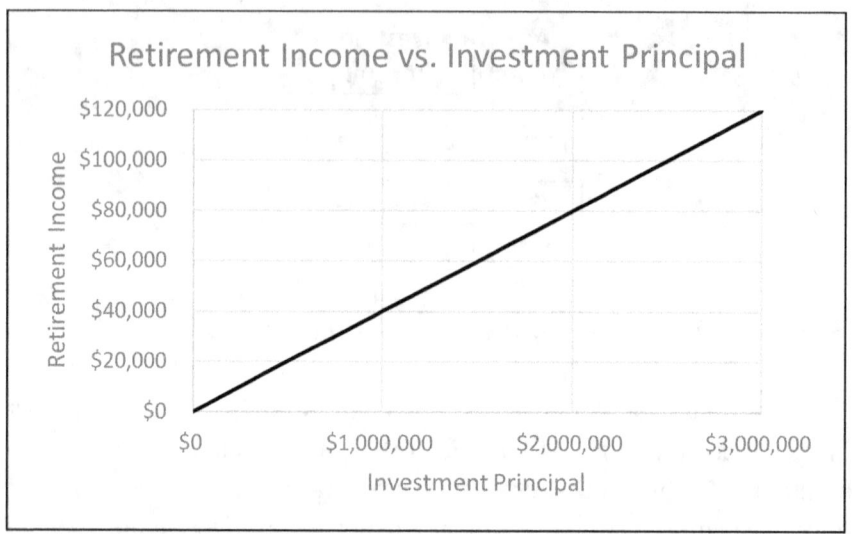

Figure 23 – Retirement Income vs. Investment principal

Making Up the Difference

If you are close to your retirement age and don't have anywhere near enough saved up to cover your expenses during retirement using the four percent rule don't panic! Applying the principals from *Chapter 4 Debt* will help set you up for a debt free life style with minimal payments, *Chapter 5 Cutting Expenses* will allow you to stretch your dollar further, and *Chapter 6 Income* will help you develop a source of supplemental income, allowing you to live a comfortable semi-retired lifestyle.

Drawdown Method

The drawdown method is a retirement strategy where you withdrawal from your investment accounts at a rate greater than the rate of growth from interest, slowly eroding the principal. Unlike the four percent rule, which provides a constant stream of income indefinitely without touching the principal, the drawdown method has a target date for when your investment accounts will likely be depleted. This method is undesirable for those seeking early retirement as you run the risk of running out of money early, leaving you with nothing to pass on to your heirs, but it does allow those without significant investments who are rapidly approaching retirement age the ability to cover their living expenses in retirement. As an example, let's assume someone 65 years of age retires and begins collecting social security. To supplement their income and cover necessary living expenses they withdrawal $23,500 per years from their 401(k) worth $250,000. The value of their investment will reach zero after just 20 years (see Figure 24 – Retirement Principal vs. Retirement Age Graph and Figure 25 – Retirement Drawdown Chart).

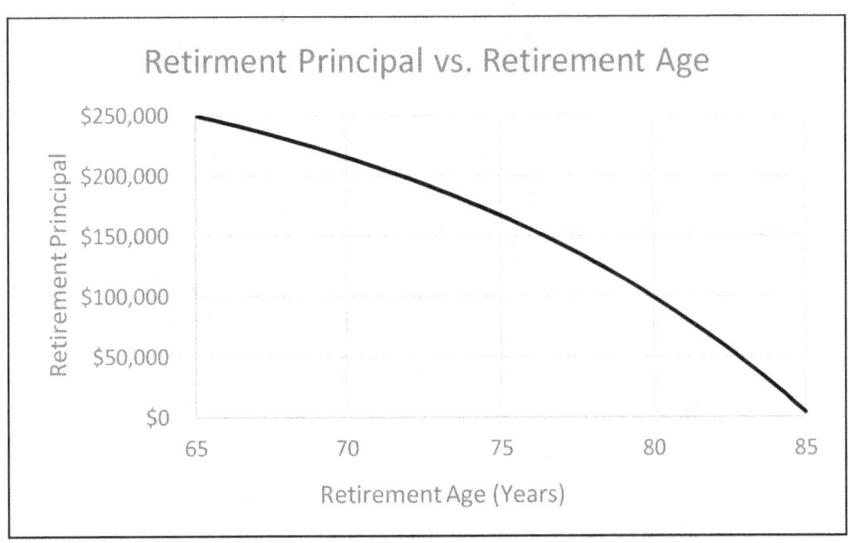

Figure 24 – Retirement Principal vs. Retirement Age Graph

Age	Principal	Interest	Withdraw
65	$250,000	$17,500	$23,500
66	$244,000	$17,080	$23,500
67	$237,580	$16,631	$23,500
68	$230,711	$16,150	$23,500
69	$223,360	$15,635	$23,500
70	$215,496	$15,085	$23,500
71	$207,080	$14,496	$23,500
72	$198,076	$13,865	$23,500
73	$188,441	$13,191	$23,500
74	$178,132	$12,469	$23,500
75	$167,101	$11,697	$23,500
76	$155,298	$10,871	$23,500
77	$142,669	$9,987	$23,500
78	$129,156	$9,041	$23,500
79	$114,697	$8,029	$23,500
80	$99,226	$6,946	$23,500
81	$82,672	$5,787	$23,500
82	$64,959	$4,547	$23,500
83	$46,006	$3,220	$23,500
84	$25,726	$1,801	$23,500
85	$4,027	$282	$4,309
86	$0	$0	$0
Interest Rate = 7%			

Figure 25 – Retirement Drawdown Chart

Social Security

Social security is a government welfare program that is funded by tax payer dollars. Signed into law in 1935 by President Franklin Roosevelt, it was originally intended to furnish financial assistance to elderly and needy individuals. Unfortunately, over the past 80 years personal savings rates have declined, and the responsibility of taking care of our own needs during retirement has shifted to reliance on the government to care for us. Despite the initial intent being to help supplement basic living expenses of only the neediest individuals, it has now become the primary (often only) retirement strategy for most middle-class families.

According to SSA.gov, 58 million beneficiaries received an average monthly benefit payment of $1,249.55, for most people this is barely enough to cover basic living expenses. You are first eligible to receive social security benefits at age 62, but at a reduced rate of 75%, with full benefits being available at age 66. You can also choose to delay your benefits until age 70, allowing you to collect 132% of the full amount (see *Figure 26 – Average and Maximum Monthly Benefits by Age* and *Figure 27 – Multiplier & Avg. Monthly Benefits vs. Age*).

Age (Years)	Multiplier	Avg. Monthly Benefits	Max. Monthly Benefits
62	75%	$937	$2,153
66	100%	$1,250	$2,687
70	132%	$1,649	$3,538

Figure 26 – Average and Maximum Monthly Benefits by Age

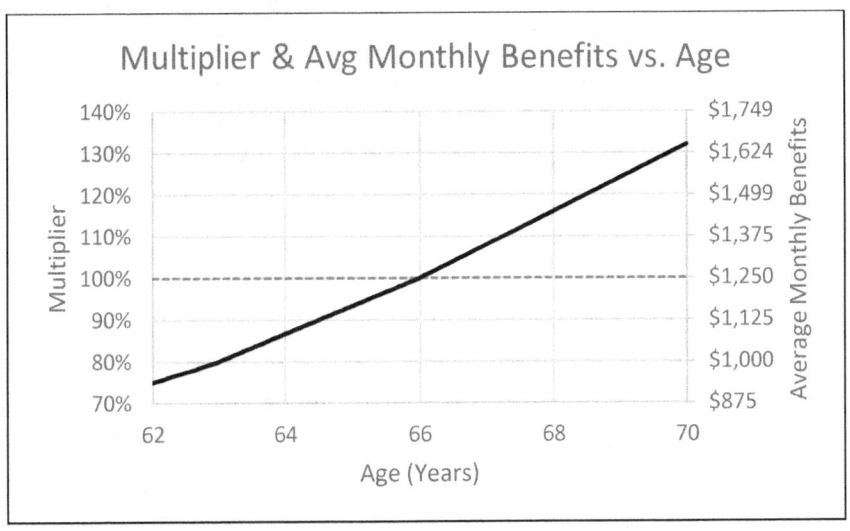

Figure 27 – Multiplier & Avg. Monthly Benefits vs. Age

If your goal is to retire early and retire rich you should focus on a path allowing you to be financially independent of others. Those who are reliant on government welfare programs are at the mercy of law makers and new regulations that can alter the benefits they are dependent on at the stroke of a pen. While social security benefits will likely not be a major part of any early retirement strategy, be sure to apply to collect your benefits when you are eligible, after all, you did pay into the program.

Downsize Your Home

Most retirees have a substantial amount of their net worth tied up in the equity of their home. For many this creates an unbalanced retirement portfolio, with hundreds of thousands of dollars stuck in a liability that can't be accessed. The value is there but because it's not liquid, it can't be used to pay bills, cover medical expenses or buy groceries. As children grow up and move out, you no longer need a 4,000-square foot home with four bedrooms, three bathrooms, a finished basement, and a two-car garage. By selling your existing large home and purchasing a smaller home in a less expensive neighborhood you can take hundreds of thousands of dollars of equity from your home and transfer it into real wealth producing assets. A smaller home will also save you thousands every year in property taxes, reduce the cost of heating and cooling, be maintenance, and cut down on the time you spend sweeping, cleaning, dusting, mowing the lawn, shoveling snow, and raking leaves. Leaving you with more time and money to visit family, travel, and live the life you always dreamed of.

Health Insurance

Most retirees receive health insurance benefits though Medicare, a Federal health insurance program that provides coverage for people who are 65 or older. One of the most common concerns of those considering early retirement is how to maintain health insurance coverage until they qualify for Medicare. Middle-class Americans typically receive health insurance benefits through their employer and are often unaware of the actual cost associated with such coverage. For those looking to retire early there are several options to bridge the gap between your desired early retirement age and when you are eligible to receive Medicare benefits.

- While rare, some employers will continue to offer health insurance coverage to employees who take early retirement. You will be grouped in with the current employees and often receiving the same benefits and pay close to the same monthly premiums. Coverage may be for a fixed period or until the former employee becomes Medicare-eligible.

- Consolidated Omnibus Budget Reconciliation Act (COBRA) allows you to pay out of pocket and maintain coverage through your former employer. Unfortunately, COBRA limits coverage to 18 months, therefore age 63.5 is the earliest you could retire using this form of coverage, making this an undesirable option.

- For those willing to transition into semi-retirement, there are many employers that offer health insurance coverage for part-time workers. Not only does this option provide you with affordable health insurance but it creates supplemental income.

- The final option is to purchase private health insurance coverage. While this is likely to be the most expensive option, it provides you with the most freedom and flexibility as you are not reliant on your former employer or forced to work part-time to cover your health care needs. Be sure to shop around and get multiple quotes as private coverage can vary greatly in price based on age, location, health, pre-existing conditions, and many other factors. To help reduce the premiums you can select a high deductible policy, which will require you to pay out of pocket to cover small medical expenses up to several thousand dollars but can save you thousands of dollars a year. To further reduce the cost a high deductible plan can be paired with Health Savings Accounts (HSA).

- An HSA is a tax-advantage savings accounts that is designed to be used with high deductible health insurance plans. Contributions are made with pre-tax dollars, grow tax free, and can be withdrawn tax free if used to cover eligible medical expenses, the perfect trifecta of tax benefits. The 2018 annual contribution limit for an individual is $3,450 and $6,900 for a family but is subject to change by the Internal Revenue Service (IRS). There is no limit to the total funds in your HSA and contributions can be made up to age 65. Unlike a 401(k) there is no requirement to make withdrawals starting at a certain age.

NOTE: The health insurance industry is constantly changing to meet new and ever-increasing health standards and frequently changing Federal and State laws. When preparing for early retirement you should seek out the advice of a knowledgeable individual within your company's human resources department or the health insurance industry to make sure you are getting the most up to date and accurate information.

TAXES

> *"The hardest thing in the world to understand is the income tax."*
> —Albert Einstein

One things we all have in common is our hatred of taxes. Our nation was founded because of excessive taxation by the British Empire, causing enraged American colonists to throw an entire shipment full of tea into Boston Harbor in 1773, eventually leading to the Revolutionary War.

Nearly 250 years later we still pay excessive taxes, but instead to our own government. A recent 2016 Gallop poll determined that 57 percent of Americans felt they paid too much income tax. Yet according to a Tax Center policy report only 45 percent of Americans actually pay taxes. Apparently, 12 percent of Americans are so confused by the tax system they don't realize they aren't even paying taxes.

But there are many ways you can lighten your tax burden and put money back in your pocket. Start by adjusting the number of allowances on your IRS Form W-4. The larger the number the less money the IRS will deduct from your pay checks. Aim for having as little refund as possible without owing any money at the end of the year. <u>An IRS tax refund is not the government giving you free money</u>, they are returning the money you overpaid throughout the year, but unlike a bank they don't pay interest on your money they held. Instead of using the government as a 0% interest savings account, take the money you earned and use it to pay down debt, invest, etc...

Some financial experts swear by always using a tax professional to do your taxes, while others feel it is unnecessary if you are completing a simple tax return and can be beneficial for developing a basic knowledge of taxes. If you run your own business, own rental properties or are dealing with a complicated financial situation such as a recent marriage, divorce or death of an immediate family member it's usually best to leave it up to the professionals.

By learning to do your own taxes you will often find extra money, avoid tax preparation fees, and learn about your personal finances. Think of preparing your taxes like an end of the year financial report card.

Below is a list of common tax deductions and write offs that many people overlook when preparing their own taxes. How many of these are you missing out on?

- State sales taxes (if your state doesn't have income tax)
- Reinvested dividends
- Charitable contributions
- Moving expense to take first job
- Child and dependent care tax credit
- Earned income tax credit
- Mileage for volunteer work
- Business expenses and losses
- Moving expenses when changing jobs
- Mortgage points
- Fees to collect investment interest and stock dividends
- Profits on the sale of your home
- Student loan interest
- Gambling losses
- Alimony
- Home mortgage interest
- Safety deposit rental cost
- Software or digital services used to prepare taxes or manage investments
- Medical expenses greater than 10% of your AGI
- Theft or disaster damage not covered by insurance
- Tuition expenses
- Work uniforms

- Business use of your home
- Unreimbursed businesses expenses such as mileage and lodging
- Teaching expenses
- Senior tax deduction

MILLIONAIRES

"To change bad habits, we must study the habits of successful role models."

—Jack Canfield

When we hear someone being described as a "millionaire" we think of red carpet celebrities, athletes, and the CEOs of big Wall Street banks. Many people assume someone with millionaire status must earn a million dollars or more per year. A millionaire by traditional definition is any person or household with million-dollar net worth (see *Figure 28 – Sample Millionaire Net Worth*).

Assets	Home Equity*	$ 300,000
	Vehicle*	$ 30,000
	401(k)	$ 600,000
	Mutual Funds	$ 150,000
	Bonds	$ 50,000
	Cash	$ 20,000
Liabilities	Mortgage	$ (100,000)
	Credit Card	$ (5,000)
	Vehicle Loan	$ (10,000)
	Student Loan	$ (10,000)
	Net Worth	**$ 1,025,000**

Figure 28 – Sample Millionaire Net Worth

*Note: Homes and vehicles do not meet the traditional definition of an asset because they do no produce wealth and cost money to maintain but can be considered assets for the purpose of calculating net worth as the equity can be accessed if sold.

On one hand, it's very inspiring to know the average millionaire isn't the CEO of some massive company, Hollywood movie star or a professional athlete. The average millionaire is often the person next door. They are engineers, accountants, lawyers, managers, plumbers, teachers, and truck drivers. Almost any middle-class family with the right attitude and knowledge can reach millionaire status. But the lackluster part of the average millionaire is the journey, they grow wealth by making sacrifices, working second jobs, taking staycations, driving used cars, cutting coupons, and making meals at home instead of eating out.

The average person with a million-dollar net worth does not look like the millionaires we see in magazine or on TV, and they don't live excessively lavish lifestyle. They have money because they get more enjoyment from saving and investing their money than they do spending it. Most people want to live like millionaires, so they can buy a big home, drive expensive sports cars, and take their yacht out on the weekend. Most of the people who do those things are either broke and faking the appearance of wealth or won't be able to maintain a millionaire net worth for long. People who become millionaires are able to do so because they don't waste their money on flashy items that depreciate in value and instead focus their habits and hobbies around creating wealth.

Statistics

Many studies have been conducted to dig deeper into the minds and lives of millionaires to determine what they have in common and highlight the factors that helped them achieve their wealthy. With over ten million millionaires in the United States there is certainly no shortage of data, below is a list of some of the more noteworthy statistics millionaires have in common:

- It's a frequent misconception that most millionaires inherit their wealth, yet studies consistently indicate over 80% of all millionaires receive little to no inheritance and are solely responsible for acquiring their wealth.

- According to a 2016 poll conducted by the Pew Research Center, 27% of Americans did not read a single book in the previous year. But millionaires have a passion for reading and learning. They read more non-fiction books that any other socio-economic group.

- According to recent research, 86% of millionaires enjoy reading compared to only 26% of the lower income families and 88% of millionaires read 30 minutes or more every day compared to just 2% of low-income families. This habit also extends to their children, with 63% of the children of wealthy parents reading two or more non-fiction books a month vs. 3% of children who grow up in low-income households.

- Millionaires are a well-educated group. Over 80% are college graduates, yet only 17% every attended a private school.

- Unlike the stereotype most millionaires don't spend their day playing golf or sipping mixed drinks on a beach. They are very hard workers, on average putting in 45-55 hours per week.

- The average millionaire is 63 years old, with their rags to riches storying taking 32 years before reaching the highly sought-after millionaire status.

- 97% of millionaires are homeowner.

- Tom Corley, author of *Rich Habits*, studied millionaires and their habits over a five-year period. He found the overwhelming majority had multiple income streams, with his multi-year study determined the following:

    I.   65% of millionaires had three or more streams of income.
    II. 45% of millionaires had four or more streams of income.
    III. 29% of millionaires had five or more streams of income.

Traits

The exact path to riches is different for each millionaire, but they do have traits in common that helped drive them to the next level of success.

Organized – Millionaires are typically very organized and live a more structured life style than most. They make schedules, plan out their day, go to bed at the same time, lay out their work clothes the night before, and have their lunch packed in the refrigerator, ready to grab in the morning. These actions are extremely important if you are not a morning person (including myself) and have trouble putting together coherent thoughts before you've had a cup of coffee. Their homes are also clean and organized. We've all spent countless hours of our lives looking for lost keys when were late for work or digging through couch cushions trying to find the TV remote. Disorganization is such a problem they sell devices you can hook to your keys and other small objects that will beep to help you locate them, of course that assumes you haven't misplace your smart phone or other device that's used to find your lost items. Millionaires, whether intentionally or not, will always keep their keys on the same hook by the garage door, their wallet is always on the night stand, their clean clothes are folded, and the dirty laundry goes directly into hampers sorted by color, not one big pile on the floor. Not only does this create a more visually appealing and stress-free household, it frees up valuable time, allowing them to be more productive in other areas of their life.

If you are naturally an unorganized person try keeping a pen and pad of paper with you. I like to put my notes on the end table next to my bed to remind me in the morning what lies ahead that day. If you're a tech person use your phone to take notes or set reminder for your to-do list. A high level of organization allows successful people to keep track of all the daily tasks that often get overlooked.

Task Oriented – They create a daily to-do list and keep it with them. As they go through the day, they cross off items that have been accomplished and write down new tasks when they think them. Keeping a list of items you have not yet accomplished may seem discouraging, but in practice produces the opposite feeling by keeping you motivated and creating a winning sense of accomplishment as you check the completed tasks off the list. I find it increases my productivity, often I will sit down at the end of the day with the intent of watching TV but will notice my to-do list and will decide to finish one or two more small tasks before heading to bed. While many of these accomplishments are small, over the course of weeks and months you will notice a difference, dirty dishes won't stay in the sink as long, the laundry will not pile up as high, and you will find it all adds up to more free time that can be used for bigger goals like starting a part-time business, reading, and spending more time with family.

Efficient – They arrange meetings back to back allowing them larger chunks of uninterrupted time. They schedule personal activities at the beginning or end of the day and eat lunch at their desk rather than going out to a restaurant. Not only does this save money, it also reduces time spent driving, standing in line, and allows them to get work done while they eat. Millionaires get the same 24 hours per day as everyone else on the planet, only they recognize time as a finite resource and choose to use it as wisely as possible.

Action Takers – Rather than wait around for something good to happen they act and take matters into their own hands. Instead of coming up with an in-depth reason why it makes sense to do the dishes tomorrow they roll up their sleeves and get to work. This is especially true for smaller tasks, they recognize that by time they think up an excuse they can already be done. They also don't let opportunities pass them by. Have you ever thought of a great idea or new invention, maybe even wrote the idea down, then did nothing about it? Time passes and you're walking down the aisles of your local big box store and you see it, "your" invention sitting on the self, someone had the same exact idea, probably even after you did, only they took action. The difference is their idea is making them rich while your idea is just a sketch on a worthless piece of paper.

Hungry – Millionaires always want more, even after accomplishing a big task, getting a raise at work or achieving a lifelong goal they never hit a quitting point. They're always chasing a moving goal post and their desire to win and be successful pushes them forward no matter the obstacle.

Visionary – They have the ability to visualize their goals and plan for the future. They visualize success and focus on filling in the gap between where they are now and where they want to be. Most people live for the here and now, but millionaires tend to see the bigger picture and understand that the actions they take now can either produce great reward or devastating consequences, either way their future is up to them.

Risk Takers – They are willing to take calculated risks, often outside of their comfort zone in search of greater reward. They understand that without taking some risk there will be no reward and only those who push themselves to their limit on a regular basis will truly be successful.

Value Seekers – They find a way to make every purchase an investment that grows in value. For items that can't be considered an investment, like food or other consumables, they do everything they can to minimize how much they spend. They view every dollar saved as a dollar earned. Someone with a millionaire mindset doesn't view a coupon just as a random piece of paper, they view it as real money they are putting right into their pocket. Cutting coupons isn't saving them money, its MAKING them money.

Real Life Millionaires

Some of the best advice comes from those who have already completed the journey. I've been fortunate enough sit down with several millionaires and had the opportunity to ask them questions about their net worth, how they invest, the obstacles they overcame, and what advice they can give to people seeking financial independence.

Millionaire Mike

Mike and his wife are 40 years old and live in Cincinnati, Ohio. He is a radiology technologist and worked at a hospital specializing in CAT scans for 17 years. He recently took a new position with a pharmaceutical research company, allowing him to still use his degree and expertise, but in an office setting, instead of directly working with patients. His wife is a technical writer and has more or less been with the same company for 17 years. Together they have two wonderful daughters that keep them busy. They love to travel and do weekend trips whenever possible. Mike has been a runner and triathlete for about seven years. He has completed seven marathons, four half Ironman triathlons, and one full Ironman triathlon, an impressive feat for someone who used to identify as a couch potato.

How did you become interested in the work you do?
I saw a program on the PBS show Nova about medicine and the MRI imaging that was featured during the show fascinated me. I had wanted to be a professional pilot since I was five years old, but after a short stint going to college for that, I decided it wasn't for me. I was always interested in science and the body, so being a radiology tech really suited my interests.

Do you have any side businesses or other sources of supplemental income?
No, but I am desperately trying to think of something to do as a side business. I can't come up with any feasible ideas and I've been thinking about it for a few years. I've thought about blogging. I really want to be location independent.

At what age did/do you plan to retire?
I'd like to retire or begin working part time at age 41 or 42.

What are your non-financial goals for retirement?
Spend more time with my children and wife, spend more time outdoors (golfing, kayaking, hiking), volunteer, create some type of business, read, and be able to travel.

At what age did you make your first million?
40

What is your net worth and how is it allocated?
1.1 million with 95% in stocks and in 5% bonds.

Do you have a target net worth or are you always trying to grow it?
Targeting 1.2 million, but I expect that with some part time work, that will continue to grow.

How did you accumulate the majority of your net worth?
All from working and saving. No inheritance or lottery winnings.

What was your biggest financial mistake you've made?
If I had to pick something, it would be the fact that we invested with Edward Jones for 10 years. We spent a lot of money on fees and commissions investing with them and I don't feel like they provided any value. I began researching investing and went completely independent about four years ago. We dipped our foot into the investing pool because of Edward Jones, so I don't completely count this as a mistake. There are plenty of resources now on the internet that a beginner investor can use to bypass these high-end brokers.

What are some big sacrifices or risks you took on your journey towards financial independence that allowed you to grow such a large fortune?
Most of the things we've done don't seem like sacrifices to us but would to most people in our society. We bought an affordable house that we could pay off in 15 years on one salary if needed. I still drive my 2003 Honda Civic and our other vehicle (that we love!) is a 2006 Toyota

Sienna. We have inexpensive cell phones from Republic wireless and no cable. I would say I didn't take any risk to allow this fortune. Most everything was calculated or at least intentional.

Do you have any frugal habits despite your large net worth?
We generally avoid going out to eat and, in fact, I don't really like eating out at restaurants much. We pack lunches, always make coffee at home, shop at Aldi, and waste almost no food. We always eat our leftovers and try to make meals in batches.

How many hours a week do you typically work?
I work 40 per week and my wife works 32 hours per week.

How many books do you read per year?
I'm always reading something, and usually have about 10 books checked out from the library at any given time. I can't say I read them all cover to cover, I read maybe 15 cover to cover per year. I read almost all non-fiction, so I'll skim, skip, find interesting parts, and then put it aside.

How many hours a day do you spend watching TV?
I try to only watch TV on the treadmill, but I'll have some weeks when I watch an hour or so a night if we find something we get in to. It's almost all documentaries on Netflix.

What has been your driving motivation for growing your wealth?
Independence. Freedom. I want to live and work on my terms and not those of an employer.

We often hear about greed and other negative aspects of money. What positive things have you been able to accomplish with your wealth?
The sense of peace is pretty amazing when you have substantial savings. You are able to make choices that you may not otherwise be comfortable with if you didn't have savings. I was able to take a chance

at a new job knowing that if it didn't work out that we would be just fine without my income.

We've been able to pay off our house in seven years which is unheard of outside of the financial independence community. This freed up a large line item in our budget that could instead be put into savings.

If you could give just one piece of advice to someone in their 20s or 30s looking to become financially independent what would it be?
My advice for younger people seeking financial independence would be to make saving and investing a game. Most people don't like personal finance because they think it's a sacrifice that they don't want to be bothered by. When you make saving and investing a game, then the process becomes enjoyable. It can actually be fun to see how low you can get your monthly food/grocery bill. It can be fun to learn how to fix your own car to save money by avoiding the mechanic. Once you see your accounts going up, up, up, then the motivation to save and invest more gives you the same dopamine hit that many people get by shopping. I actually get a rush when I make a nice deposit into my Vanguard account!

Any final thoughts for those seeking financial independence?
<u>Use the library often</u> – Not only can you get free books, movies, and music, but you can really spark interest in a variety of topics by perusing the library shelves. I've improved and motivated myself so much because of my library habit. Our local library can deliver any book in the system to your local library, so I'm always reserving books through their app. There's no harm since everything is free!

<u>Learn a little more every day and get a little better every week</u> – Don't be intimidated by investing. Just vow to yourself that you will learn a little more every day. There are endless resources on YouTube, finance blogs, and podcasts related to financial independence. Also, try to do one thing that improves your finances every week. For example, see if you can get better insurance rates one week, look into cheaper phones

the next week, critique your food/restaurant spending and develop a plan to reduce them the week after that. 52 changes in one year will almost assuredly save you hundreds if not thousands per year.

<u>Automate saving</u> – This is crucial. You won't even miss the money if it comes right out of your paycheck or if it automatically comes out of your bank account.

Millionaire Gary

Gary is a 63-year-old self-made entrepreneur and investor who lives with his wife in sunny southern Florida. He owns and operates 3,500 rental units including multiple mobile home parks, apartment complexes, and commercial properties. His favorite hobbies are collecting classic cars, boating, and just about anything with a motor.

How did you become interested in the work you do?
I always wanted to work for myself and be my own boss. When I was younger I worked at a bank for about a year while I took college classes, which my company was paying for. But I just couldn't see myself wearing a suit and tie every day for the rest of my life. I gave my two weeks notice and bought a gas station after I quit, that was the business my father had been in his whole life. Eventually I sold the gas station and went in with a business partner to buy a mobile home park. I've slowly and steadily been growing my business ever since.

Do you have any side businesses or other sources of supplemental income?
I have numerous sources of income. I build and sell homes, manage rental properties, renovate and flip existing properties, operate a warehouse, buy and sell collectable cars, and at one point I was even in the dry ice business.

At what age did/do you plan to retire?
I have no plans to really retire. I like what I do and enjoy keeping busy. I have friends who are retired that play golf all day long, I don't know how they do it. I enjoy constantly chasing the next deal, that's half the fun.

What are your non-financial goals for retirement?
I would like to travel more and visit the world. I'm planning to take a trip to Japan sometime soon.

Retire Early, Retire Rich

At what age did you make your first million?
I made my first million at age 30, it was a goal my business partner and I set for ourselves back then.

What is your net worth and how is it allocated?
My current net worth is around 60 million, of which approximately 40 million is in real estate and 20 is in stocks and miscellaneous assets.

Do you have a target net worth or are you always trying to grow it?
I am content with that I have now. I know many people who are always looking for more, it's an ego thing, but there is always someone who has more money than you. If you're always comparing yourself to others you will never be happy with what you have.

How did you accumulate the majority of your net worth?
Most of my wealth was accumulated through the sale and management of rental properties. I'm very thankful to have had such good fortune doing what I enjoy.

What was your biggest financial mistake you've made?
Buying raw land to develop right before the housing bubble popped. I own parcels of land that over a decade later I will take a haircut on when I finally sell.

What are some big sacrifices or risks you took on your journey towards financial independence that allowed you to grow such a large fortune?
My family life often suffered from being extremely busy. I also took large financial risks early on by taking out tens of thousands of dollars in personal loans to buy rental properties, if something would have gone wrong it would have been financially devastating. I can remember having to put $30,000 on a credit card one winter to pay the utilities for a mobile home park, those were nerve-racking times I'll never forget.

Do you have any frugal habits despite your large net worth?
I still cut coupons from the Sunday newspaper and shop the two for one deals. I was raised this way by my parents and never changed.

How many hours a week do you typically work?
Currently 40-50 hours a week but there were times when I was growing my business that I worked significantly more than that.

How many books do you read per year?
None.

How many hours a day do you spend watching TV?
Maybe a few hours.

What has been your driving motivation for growing your wealth?
I currently have no desire to grow my wealth. But when I was younger my goal was always to take something, make it better, and make money doing it. I like chasing the next deal and have always felt money was made on the buy, not the sale.

We often hear about greed and other negative aspects of money. What positive things have you been able to accomplish with your wealth?
It has allowed me to donate to charities and help those in need. My wife and I have our estate setup to create trust funds for numerous non-profit charitable organizations.

If you could give just one piece of advice to someone in their 20s or 30s looking to become financially independent what would it be?
Do what you enjoy, it's easy to work hard, stay focused, and be successful when you're doing what you love. All the money in the world won't make up for having to do a job you hate every day.

Any final thoughts for those seeking financial independence?
Don't let failure get you down, use it as a learning experience and grow from it. The very first rental property I bought was a mobile home and it was a disaster, it was in a rough part of town, we had terrible tenants, and we eventually sold it without making any money. But what I did get out of that experience was valuable financial knowledge and business skills. If I would have given up after that first attempt I wouldn't be where I am today.

Millionaire Greg

Greg is a Certified Public Accountant who works for a large media company, and lives with his wife and kids in Cleveland, Ohio. His resume includes working for several of the top accounting firms in the country and he has had the opportunity to work with countless successful clients, providing him first-hand knowledge on handling and growing wealth. His favorite hobby is fitness and exercise. He believes health is the key towards productivity and your money is of no use if you don't live long enough to enjoy it.

How did you become interested in the work you do?
I originally wanted to be a cop, but my parents wanted me to go to college, so I compromised and decided to work for the FBI, which at the time required either an accounting or law degree. After several internships and numerous job offers in hand my senior year of college I stuck with accounting.

Do you have any side businesses or other sources of supplemental income?
I, along with several business partners purchased a company called MTech, a sewer and street safety and maintenance equipment company.

At what age did/do you plan to retire?
Around age 65. I could retire earlier but I prefer to keep my regular income until all my kids are finished with college.

What are your non-financial goals for retirement?
To one day be able to travel, maybe own a vacation home, and have the time to volunteer.

At what age did you make your first million?
I made my first million about ten years ago, but I don't track my net worth that closely, so I don't have an exact date.

Retire Early, Retire Rich

What is your net worth and how is it allocated?
My net worth is over a million. Off the top of my head I would say its distributed approximated 25% in real estate, 50% in retirement accounts, and 25% in miscellaneous assets.

Do you have a target net worth or are you always trying to grow it?
Yes, I have a target net worth, but I don't define it numerically, it's more about what I will need for a comfortable lifestyle in retirement.

How did you accumulate the majority of your net worth?
Most is a result of my day job, which has allowed me to regularly invest in a 401(k) and take advantage of good stock market growth over time.

What was your biggest financial mistake you've made?
The biggest mistake I made was cashing out my 401(k) plans when I was younger and changed jobs. I would likely have a much larger net worth now if I would have just rolled over the accounts to my new company's 401(k).

What are some big sacrifices or risks you took on your journey towards financial independence that allowed you to grow such a large fortune?
I invested in MTech back in January of 2009 right after the recession. It was a big risk to take during a down economy, but it paid off in the long run.

Do you have any frugal habits despite your large net worth?
I don't cut coupons or anything like that, I prefer to focus my energy elsewhere. I think avoiding stupid and wasteful habits like gambling, drinking, smoking, and other vices has the biggest impact on your financial situation. If you can divert money away from wasteful spending and towards more productive uses it will have a significant impact on your net worth.

You should also avoid trying to keep up with the Joneses, I know far too many people who will go out and buy a brand-new Jaguar just because someone down the street bought one, even though the Chevy they were driving suited them just fine. Not to mention that new automobiles are one of the worst possible investments.

How many hours a week do you typically work?
Typically, 50 hours a week.

How many books do you read per year?
Maybe one, I read more articles and newspapers. Books are a great source of knowledge and help keep you sharp, I wish I had more time to read.

What has been your driving motivation for growing your wealth?
To provide for my family and be able to retire comfortably.

We often hear about greed and other negative aspects of money. What positive things have you been able to accomplish with your wealth?
I think it's important that we do right by other people and make every effort to better the lives of those around us, at the end of our journey we don't get to take money with us. My wealth has enabled me to help others in my community. My church and my children's school are where I focus my giving. But there are many ways to give back to others, you can donate your time, your talent or your treasure. Not everyone has all three, if you don't yet have treasure, instead donate your time or your talent.

If you could give just one piece of advice to someone in their 20s or 30s looking to become financially independent what would it be?
Start thinking about and saving for your future as early as possible and stay disciplined no matter what happens. As time passes compound interest will cause the value of your investments to snowball.

Any final thoughts for those seeking financial independence?
My company automatically starts all new employees out at a 3% contribution rate to their 401(k), it's not a lot but it better than nothing and causes people to get excited about investing and gets them to start thinking about their future. The biggest step is just opening an account and starting to contribute, it's simple after that.

Millionaire Paul

Paul is a retired police officer, having finished a 30-year career. He lives with his wife, a retired school teacher in a small rural community in the Midwest. Despite being retired he often feels busier than ever. He spends much of his free time watching his grandkids. Paul doesn't travel much, as he prefers the comfort of his own home where he enjoys numerous hobbies including fishing, hunting, and wood working.

How did you become interested in the work you do?
I like working with people and wanted a job that wasn't routine, I didn't want to work at a desk all day. Being a police officer allowed me to give back to the community while doing something I enjoyed.

Do you have any side businesses or other sources of supplemental income?
I worked private security on my days off when I was younger but haven't done that in years. My wife used to work as a camp counselor during summer beak before we had kids.

At what age did/do you plan to retire?
My wife and I both retired around age 55.

What are your non-financial goals for retirement?
Volunteer and spend more time with our children and grandchildren.

At what age did you make your first million?
Probably in our early 50s but we didn't realize it at the time.

What is your net worth and how is it allocated?
Most of our wealth is tied up in pensions because we were both government employees. According to our financial advisor the combined present value of our pensions is right around one million dollars. The rest of our wealth is in the equity of our paid for home, our two cars, and mutual funds we purchased over the years.

Do you have a target net worth or are you always trying to grow it?
No, we never had an exact dollar amount in mind, our goal was always just to be able to retire comfortably. Being a millionaire was not really part of the plan.

How did you accumulate the majority of your net worth?
Just by working hard, saving, and staying out of debt

What was your biggest financial mistake you've made?
Not investing more when we were younger. I think knowing we had a guaranteed pension allowed us to sleep easy at night, but it also caused us to overlook opportunities to invest and grow our wealth in other ways. Just because you have a pension doesn't mean you can't invest on your own in the stock market.

That and buying a camper we rarely used and sold for a fraction of what we paid for it just a few years later. Really wish I could have that money back.

What are some big sacrifices or risks you took on your journey towards financial independence that allowed you to grow such a large fortune?
We both sacrificed free time when we were younger before we had kids. My wife could have stayed home during the summer and relaxed but instead she worked. I worked a lot of weekends and picked up extra shifts when I could, that was time away from my family. We also didn't spend on many luxury items, we didn't vacation much, and never owned a new car until a few years ago.

Do you have any frugal habits despite your large net worth?
We still do all the frugal cost saving things we did when we were younger. Honestly, we don't feel "rich" and in my experience those that act rich usually aren't.

How many hours a week do you typically work?
None now. Probably 40-50 when we were working.

How many books do you read per year?
Me? Zero. My wife probably reads a dozen or more. See will stop by the library maybe once a month.

How many hours a day do you spend watching TV?
We rarely watch TV when the weather is nice. During the winter we watch way more than we should.

What has been your driving motivation for growing your wealth?
To make sure my family was taken care, to have a comfortable retirement, and to know that I won't be a financial burden to my kids when I'm older and grayer than I already am.

We often hear about greed and other negative aspects of money. What positive things have you been able to accomplish with your wealth?
I'm able to donate regularly to my church, which is something I often couldn't do when I was younger, and money was tighter. I can remember picking change out of the cup holder in my car before going inside just so I had something to put in the offering basket. Now if there is a young couple with kids next to me I'll toss in extra and let them know they're covered.

We were also able to help pay for our kid college, which is a luxury we never had, and has given them a jump start on life.

If you could give just one piece of advice to someone in their 20s or 30s looking to become financially independent what would it be?
Don't buy stupid stuff you can't afford and don't really need. I think a lot of young folks have given up on the American dream, they think it's no longer possible, especially since the last recession hit. Honestly

that's sad, because it is still possible, but only if they stop buying the latest smartphone and start saving for their future.

Any final thoughts for those seeking financial independence?
We never had large incomes, but we lived within our means, and didn't compare ourselves to others. We had pensions which are not very common these days other than government jobs, but the same thing can be done in the private sector with a 401(k), you just have to make saving a priority.

BETTER YOURSELF

"Taking the first step is the difference between actually pursuing your passion and just dreaming about it."
—Jack Canfield

Success is a combination of knowledge and the actions you take to achieve your goals. As simple as that sounds, it took me nearly a decade to figure that out.

As a new college graduate in my early 20s, I remember standing in the parking lot at my school, having just finished packing my car with the last of my belongings from my apartment. Turning back towards the main buildings on campus with a scrunched-up graduation gown in one hand and a cap and tassel in the other, I breathed a sigh of relief and said to myself...

"I did it! I'm done! I'm finally done learning!"

I may have just earned a college degree, but that was quite possibly the most foolish statement I've ever made. If you truly desire to be successful, you can never stop learning and must always be working to increase your knowledge and skill base.

In the years after college I started my career and got married to my wonderful wife. Together we talked about our future and all the big dreams we had, but as the years passed by, our dreams didn't seem to be coming any closer to reality. After years of blindly taking steps towards what I hoped would be a desirably future, I found myself desperate for motivation and guidance, so for the first time since college I picked up a book and started to read. My wife did a double take as she saw me sitting quietly in the corner with a book, she must have thought I was sick. But that book, *The Success Principles*, by Jack Canfield changed my attitude towards learning and how I viewed success. I no longer sit back and just hope for what I want to come true, instead I take intentional and deliberate actions on a daily basis to achieve my goals.

Relationships

Motivational speaker, Jim Rohn, once said:

"You are the average of the five people you spend the most time with."

I believe most of us have far more than five people in our lives that influence us, but the core of the message is that we are influenced by and unknowingly emulate those who we spend time with. If you want to be successful, you need to surround yourself with successful, positive thinking, intelligent, and like-minded individuals that are motivated to better their lives. People like this are a wealth of knowledge and will provide you with various tips, tricks, and opportunities for increasing your wealth and help you overcome obstacles along your journey towards financial independence.

As you grow into wealth and develop a new lifestyle with increasingly lofty goals, you may find that people you are close with may not align with or support your current values and aspirations. It is even possible that some may grow to resent you, become jealous of your wealth or simply not understand why you have changed. While some will offer praise and support for your accomplishment, others may mock or criticize your actions. You shouldn't go out of your way to avoid those who do not agree with or support your goals; however, it is important to not let their opinions negatively influence your actions or make you feel guilty for your success. They are witnessing your success through a narrow lens, and only see the wealth you have created, not the long hours spend at the office, personal sacrifices made, risks taken, or the time and money donated to help others.

Mentorships

As you start your journey of wealth building and early retirement, take the path well-travelled by following in the footsteps of someone who has already arrived at the destination. A good mentor is a knowledgeable individual with experience and the willingness to share their wisdom with others. A mentor may be older or younger than the person they are mentoring, but the one thing they all have in common is their ability to provide you with the skills, wisdom, and the motivation necessary to guide you towards your goals.

Most people learn by trial and error but having a mentor can save you the hardship and loss of having to learn firsthand. We all have that friend, the one who comes to us with their problems again and again. Wise and thoughtful people will give them advice, yet they never seem to take it or make meaningful changes in their life. The answer to their problems may be right in front of them, and to you the answer is obvious, but because they learn through trial and error, not by seeking out advice and guidance, they are unable to learn and grow until they go through the process of failing, looking back, analyzing what went wrong, and finally devising a plan to avoid that pain of failure in the future. While this method works, it is slow, costly, and not best suited for growing wealth quickly. Instead seek out a mentor, tap into their knowledge, and learn from their mistakes for free.

How do you find a mentor?

When seeking out a mentor for building wealth be extra cautious, a lot of people appear to be wealthy from a far, but a big home and a luxury car in the driveway is not an indicator of wealth, in many cases it is the opposite. Constant pressure from society and the desire for keeping up with the Joneses can make it difficult to identify those who are truly wealthy and those who are just living a lie of a life financed by debt.

Start by identifying individuals who have already achieved the goal you are pursuing. Successful people love sharing their story and are almost always willing to give like-minded and motivated individuals valuable advice. The mistake most people make is expecting more than just advice from their mentor. Wealthy people are constantly approached by individuals trying to gain access to their wealth in one form or another, often on a daily basis. By letting them know you are not seeking their money, but instead looking for wisdom and guidance they will be more willing to help you. Never ask a mentor for a loan, or to invest in a business idea you have. That is not the role of a mentor. If you need funding meet with a bank to acquire a loan, seek out investors or business partners. Never go up to a potential mentor and ask:

> "Will you be my mentor?"

Most people will translate this as:

> "I'm extremely lazy and can't solve problems on my own. Can you just tell me how to be rich, do all of the work for me, and hold my hand the entire time just in case I get scared?"

A good mentorship can last years or even a lifetime, no successful person with a busy schedule will make that kind of commitment to a person, especially if they barely know you. Instead start simple, ask a few questions about them, but don't be too chatty, it is better to just get to the point and ask the questions you need to know, rather than wasting their valuable time with unnecessary pleasantries. Try some variation of the following:

> "You seem like a very successful and inspiring person, I always wondered how you got started in your career?"

This compliments their success, lets them know you look up to them, that you are passionate about a common interest, and are willing to listen and learn. A good mentorship is like a friendship, it can't be forced, it must be allowed to grow organically over time, allowing both parties to trust the other and form a strong bond.

Eventually there will come a day when someone notices your success and asks for guidance. Remember your humble beginnings, the success your mentor helped you achieve, and take the opportunity to pay that generosity forward.

Toxic Relationships

Time is a precious asset and should not be wasted, especially on people who do nothing but drag you down. Toxic relationships creep into our lives often undetected, erode our confidence and limit our ability to be successful. When possible attempt to end or at least limit your exposure to toxic relationships. In situations where you are unable or unwilling to end a relationship, such as with a close family member it's important to set clear boundaries.

Toxic relationships are usually easy for outsiders to spot, but our personal connection with a family member or lifelong friend may cause us to make excuses, overlook serious issues, and see everything through rose colored glasses. Here are some common indicators to help you identify toxic relationships in your life:

- Keeping score
- When everything feels like a competition
- Passive-aggression
- Controlling behavior
- Blaming others for their failures
- Lack of boundaries
- Constantly asking for money
- Dwelling on the past
- Having nothing positive to say
- Unsupportive of your goals

Giving

Many of us were brought up to believe that wealthy people are greedy and self-centered. They supposedly care only about themselves and how they can steal money from others. Yet successful people are usually some of the most generous, selfless, giving people, you will ever meet. Those who try to cheat, steal and lie their way into wealth will never be successful. They will lose repeat customers, build a bad reputation, burn bridges with business partners, and in some cases even end up in jail. Even those who do not break laws or step over moral boundaries will be severely limited as their desire to be stingy and hoard their wealth will push others away. It will prevent them from developing meaningful relationships and cause them to miss out on opportunities to growth their wealth and live a happy life.

Generosity isn't limited to just our social interactions. Giving to others physically and emotionally changes how we think by activating the reward center of our brains, causing a happy and rewarding feeling produced by the release of dopamine, oxytocin, and endorphins. These are the same chemicals our body releases when we see a loved one or hug an adorable puppy. By helping others it helps us build emotional bonds and develop trust in others and ourselves.

Being generous creates a virtuous cycle, where the more you give, the more you will earn, and the more you earn the more you can give. Even small acts of kindness and generosity can compound into unimaginable levels of reward.

Just remember that too much of a good thing can have a negative impact. When it comes to giving it's important not to give too much of yourself or your money. The best piece of advice I received on helping others was on an airplane during the pre-flight safety briefing. As the airplane taxied to the runway the stewardess held up the bright yellow oxygen mask and instructed the cabin:

"Secure your oxygen mask first, before you assist others."

These instructions are given because without oxygen, your ability to help those around you on the plane is nearly impossible and you will likely do more harm than good.

The same principal applies to everyday generosity. Your priority in life must be to take care of yourself and make sure your basic needs are met first. Only when you are happy, healthy, and well rested can you most effectively help others who are in need. This means occasionally you will have to say no to some requests for help. If you're still in debt you can't help a family member out with a loan, if you're working 80+ hours a week you don't have time to babysit your friend's kids or mow your neighbor's lawn while they're on vacation. Stretching yourself too thin will limit your ability to give your best, prevent you from helping others in the future, and quite possibly create a situation where you yourself will need assistance to get through the hard times created by over extending your generosity.

Attitude

Your level of success is directly related to your attitude. A negative attitude will drive away friends and family, drain you of energy, and overwhelm you with stress. A positive attitude will lead to increased happiness, more successful relationships, and higher productivity. When you develop a positive attitude, you will become more optimistic, feel less stressed, be healthier, and will be able to think of a positive future and focus on long term goals.

Most people don't question the control we all have over our body but what may be surprising to some is the amount of control we have over our mind and our ability to change our feelings and choose our actions. Every day we all make choices, we choose to get up and go to work, we choose what we will eat that day, how we will spend our money, and what we will do with our free time. Every choice we make will produce either positive or negative results in our lives.

Have you ever wondered why people react differently to the same situation?

If someone is taking their dog for a walk, why is it that one person will go up to the dog to pet it while another will be fearful and go out of their way to avoid the animal?

Our brains are designed to quickly process the massive amounts of information we constantly take in through our senses and process it through emotional filters in our subconscious brain that are wired based on past experiences and how we were raised by our friends and family. This setup allows us to effortlessly react to our surroundings while being able to walk, talk, and chew bubble gum, all at the same time. But our conscious brain has the final say, we can choose to change our natural reaction, hold back negative feelings, and instead focus on the positives of any given situation.

If you experience rejection, you brain will naturally seek out a similar past experience of rejection and produce the same emotions previously used for that event. As a result, being denied a promotion at work as an adult might instantly bring back memories of being cut from a sports team as a child, producing feelings such as sadness or frustration. But our conscious brain has the ability to override the subconscious, allowing us to focus on positive thoughts, and produce a positive reaction and attitude for the event.

Let's consider an example of someone who is living paycheck-to-paycheck, finding themselves yet again at the end of another month without enough money to pay the bills. Their natural subconscious reaction might be the feelings of depression, disappointment or defeat. They will rationalize their negative feelings by saying:

> "I've been broke my whole life, nothing will ever change, I should just give up!"

They should instead focus on positive emotions by visualize their long-term goals and refusing to let a single negative event define their future.

No person or object can make you feel happy or sad. How you choose to interpret and react to a specific situation is unique to you. Having a positive attitude is as simple as choosing to think positively, it's so easy yet most people are never told they have such control. As negative thoughts enter your mind, change direction and instead think of being happy, fulfilled, and achieving your goals. Once you grasp the idea that you have control over your mind and your actions, your ability to think positively, stay focused, and work towards your goals will become significantly easier.

Ways to create a positive attitude are:

- Visualize yourself achieving your goals
- Break up large overwhelming tasks into smaller more manageable pieces
- Use positive uplifting language in every day conversations
- Surround yourself by people with positive attitudes
- Make a list every day of five things you are thankful for
- Learn to laugh and smile even during stressful times
- Read stories and quotes for daily inspiration
- Focus on making mistakes a learning experience

Negative behaviors to avoid:

- Comparing your life to others
- Negative self-talk such as *"I can't…"* or *"I'll never be able to…"*
- Reliving past failures
- Fear of the unknown
- Having unrealistic expectations
- Over analyzing a situation

Avoid Time Wasters

With unlimited time, there is potential for one to acquire unlimited wealth, unfortunately our time is finite, making the little time we do have a scarce and valuable resource.

Yet people waste time like they have an unlimited supply of it. We all spend copious amounts of time watching TV, playing video games or participating in other unproductive activities. Sure, we all need to relax on occasion, but this book isn't titled *"Five New Ways to Relax"*. Who hasn't picked up their phone to respond to a text message and an hour later are still looking at their phone, browsing social media, watching funny videos, etc... According to a 2016 Nielsen study, the average American watches nearly 4.3 hours of TV a day which equates to roughly 30 hours per week. What could you accomplish with an extra 30 hours a week?

Even a small reduction, say one hour per day would provide you with the time necessary to read a few chapters of a book, meditate, take the dog for a walk, catch up on rest, sort through that stack of bills pilling up on the kitchen table or work on a part time business.

The first step to gaining back your time is identifying where it is wasted. For most people it's usually their smart phone, tv, computer or other source of media, but it doesn't always have to be an electronic device. People can also be one the biggest wasters of our time, such as the neighbor who wants to talk about the weather or the co-worker who waits until the end of the day as you're walking out the door to ask a question. Maybe it's the friend you haven't seen in years who still calls whenever they need to move furniture (because they need to borrow your pickup truck) but they never seem to be available to return the favor when you need something.

Other time wasters are in the habits we've done our entire lives. I used to wait until the last minute to do my Christmas shopping. I would fight the crowd, wait in lines, and spend countless hours driving all over the city looking for the right gift. One year I decided it was time to work smarter, not harder. Just as the internet can save you money by allowing you to find the lowest price possible it also allows you to shop from the convenience of your home. In less time than it would take you to drive to the mall and find a good parking spot, you can have all of your gifts ordered and a few days later they arrive on your door step, pre-boxed and ready to be wrapped. No hassle, no headache, saving you time, and money.

Recognize (and if necessary avoid) the people, objects, and activities that are holding you back and causing you to be unproductive with your time. Don't be afraid to tell your friend you are too busy to help them move or that your co-work's question will just have to wait until the next morning. Your time is valuable, start treating it that way.

Pause and take a minute to reflect over the past week.

What time wasters can you identify?

What actions will you take to avoid these in the future?

What will you do with your extra time?

Focus

Most people spend far too much time worry about aspects of their lives they have absolutely no control over or those that have minimal impact on a daily basis. A perfect example is politics, every few years during a major election cycle we are bombarded with political ads, telling us some candidate running for a political office will make our lives better if we vote for them instead of the other candidate. All we have to do is check the box next to their name on the ballet and all of the world's problems will be solved. People get fired up, they post on social media, they argue with their friends and family about who to vote for, some even take time off from work and spend money they don't have to attend campaign rallies to support candidates who could probably pay for the cost of their campaign themselves. Many will argue that if their candidate gets elected, their lives will be better, taxes, healthcare, and the price of goods and services will magically become cheaper overnight. I'm not saying don't vote, you should vote, but this is one of those instances where you need to ignore the bigger picture and focus in on the details. The biggest return on the investment of your time is in yourself. Politicians have been promising to make voters wealthy since the first democratic elections took place in ancient Greece, yet two and a half millennia later they have yet to fulfill that promise. Stop hoping and praying someone else will fix your problems and make you wealthy and instead take control of your fate.

You, and only you, have the ability to better your life, retire decades before your peers, and create wealth that will last for generations. When you finish this book, will you turn on the TV and watch another predictable reality TV show or will you sit down and write out a budget or think of an idea for a side business?

Your future and your success are entirely up to you and the time to take action is now!

FURTHER READING

The citations in this section are suggestions for further reading and acknowledgement of work. If you make it your goal to read just one of the books on this list per month, in one year you will have obtained more financial knowledge than the average person will in their entire life time. These books are excellent resources that will expand not only your finance skills but help motivate you to retire early and retire rich.

Automatic Millionaire, by David Bach
How to Win Friends & Influence People, by Dale Carnegie
Millionaire Success Habits, by Dean Graziosi
Money Master the Game, by Tony Robbins
Rich Dad Poor Dad, by Robert T. Kiyosaki
Richest Man in Babylon, by George S. Clason
The 4-Hour Workweek, by Timothy Ferriss
The 7 Habits of Highly Effective People, by Stephen R Covey
The Millionaire Next Door, by Thomas J. Stanley and William D. Danko
The Success Principles, by Jack Canfield
The Total Money Makeover, by Dave Ramsey
Think and Grow Rich, by Napoleon Hill

Retire Early, Retire Rich

INDEX

A

action, 3-4, 8, 129-130, 149-150, 155, 157 160
age 55 rule, 100
American Dream, 3, 9, 12, 49, 147
assets, 49-51, 62, 67, 69-70, 72, 118, 125
attitude, 3, 126, 155-157

B

balance, 8-10
bank, 17, 46-47, 56, 75, 79, 83, 91, 121, 125, 136
bankruptcy, 1, 76
behavior, 1, 34, 153, 157
bonus, 15, 37, 39, 53-54
budget, 21-22, 32, 76, 160

C

calculator, 107
cars, 16-17, 41, 50, 69, 126
cash, 22, 31, 45-46, 69
college, 4, 7, 12, 18, 72-73, 149
compound interest, 18, 54-56, 79
credit cards, 12, 16, 22-23, 31

D

debt, 1, 4, 5-6, 10, 15-20, 46, 54, 73, 85, 112, 114, 121
consolidation, 17-18
credit card, 4, 5, 16, 22
student loan, 12-13, 18-20
donate, 4, 139, 143, 147
drawdown method, 114-115

E

early withdrawal, 46, 59, 62, 98, 100-101, 107-108
penalty, 100-101, 107-108
education, 37, 72-74
emergency fund, 45-46, 113
expenses, 7, 10, 21-36, 42, 45-47, 97-105, 113-123
cutting, 21-36, 114

F

failure, 1, 4, 140, 151, 153, 157
fees, 25, 47, 49-50, 61, 63, 64-66, 73, 77, 87, 98, 122, 133
finance
personal, 1-2, 10, 122, 135
financial freedom, 3, 16
financial independence, 4, 8-9, 58, 62, 97, 131, 133, 135, 138, 140, 142, 146, 148, 150
five-year rule, 78, 87
focus, 118, 130, 139, 155, 159
food, 10, 22-23, 113
eating out, 22-23

planning meals, 23
four percent rule, 111-113

G

giving, 3-8, 35-36, 143, 154
goals, 3-6, 10, 61, 107, 129, 133, 137, 141, 145, 149-157

H

health insurance, 118-120
hobbies, 41-43, 70
home
   buying tips, 88-93
   downsize, 118
   insurance, 93
   maintenance, 93
   ownership, 75-95
   vacation, 50, 94, 111, 141

I

income, 37-43
   passive, 40-41, 73
   supplemental, 39-40, 42, 114, 119, 132, 137, 141, 145
inflation, 46, 64-65, 70-71, 101
investing, 11, 18, 20, 41, 45-46, 53-74, 76, 97, 111, 126, 133, 135, 144, 146
   529 savings plan, 72-73
   alternative, 69-70
   bonds, 68-69, 72, 101, 133
   index fund, 60, 62, 66, 101
   mutual Fund, 58, 60, 62-69, 72, 98, 101, 110
   pensions, 57-58, 62, 72, 98, 145-146
   precious metals, 69-71
   Roth 401(k), 58-61, 107-109
   Roth IRA, 60-61, 100-105, 107-109
   stocks, 41, 46, 49, 56-57, 62, 66, 69, 71, 133, 138
   thrift savings plan, 61-62
   traditional 401(k), 58-60, 98, 100-105
   traditional IRA, 60-61, 98, 100-105

K

kids, 31-33

L

liabilities, 49-51
lifestyle creep, 15
luxury, 13, 113, 146-147, 151

M

marriage, 7, 10, 76, 121
Medicare, 97, 118-119
mentorship, 151-153
middle-class, 2, 6, 7, 16, 45, 49-50, 54, 75, 98, 117-118, 126
millionaires, 125-148
mortgage
   30 vs. 15 year, 79
motivation, 3-10, 92, 134-135, 139, 143, 147, 149-151

N
negotiation, 25-29

Q
qualified distributions, 99

P
past & present, 11-13
purpose, 6-8

R
raise, 15-16, 37-38, 76, 130
real estate, 40, 69, 88, 138, 142
recession, 12, 68-71, 111, 142
refinancing, 83-87
relationships, 9, 150, 154-155
   toxic 153
renting vs. owning, 77-78
retail therapy, 22
retirement
   early retirement, 6, 8, 16, 45, 58, 63, 97-120, 151
   gap, 97-98
rollover, 104, 108, 109
Roth IRA conversion ladder, 100-104

S
saving, 45-47
   CD, 46
   emergency fund, 45-46
   money market, 47

SEPP, 105-108
Social Security, 97, 115-118
stock market, 54-58, 64, 67, 69-70, 77, 142, 146
stress, 10, 22, 23, 36, 38, 41, 128, 155
student loans, 12, 18-20

T
taxes, 49-50, 59, 63-64, 67-68, 72-73, 100-102 121-123
   property, 77, 90, 118
tax advantage, 58, 60, 98-99, 101
tax loss harvesting, 67-68
time, 158-159

V
vacation, 4, 7, 10, 15, 30, 53, 101, 146, 155
Vanguard, 63, 135
visualize, 4, 130

W
Wall Street, 12, 57, 125
warranty, 29-30

www.ingramcontent.com/pod-product-compliance
Lightning Source LLC
Chambersburg PA
CBHW052255220526
45471CB00001B/354